CDs, Super Glue, and Salsa

series 2

HOW EVERYDAY PRODUCTS ARE MADE

CDs, Super Glue, and Salsa

series 2

HOW EVERYDAY PRODUCTS ARE MADE

Volume 2: K-Z

Edited by:
Kathleen L. Witman,
Kyung Lim Kalasky
& Neil Schlager

AN IMPRINT OF GALE

CDs, Super Glue, and Salsa: How Everyday Products Are Made, Series 2
Edited by Kathleen L. Witman, Kyung Lim Kalasky, and Neil Schlager

Staff

Jane Hoehner, *U·X·L Developmental Editor*
Betz Des Chenes, *Contributing U·X·L Developmental Editor*
Carol DeKane Nagel, *U·X·L Managing Editor*
Thomas L. Romig, *U·X·L Publisher*

Margaret A. Chamberlain, *Permissions Specialist (Pictures)*

Shanna Heilveil, *Production Assistant*
Evi Seoud, *Assistant Production Manager*
Mary Beth Trimper, *Production Director*

Mark Howell (with Pamela A.E. Galbreath), *Page and Cover Designer*
Cynthia Baldwin, *Product Design Manager*
Barbara J. Yarrow, *Graphic Services Supervisor*
Pam Hayes, *Photography Coordinator*
Randy Bassett, *Imaging Supervisor*

The Graphix Group, *Typesetting*

Library of Congress Cataloging-in-Publication Data
CD's, superglue, and salsa : how everyday products are made : series II / [Kathleen Witman, Kyung-Sun Lim, and Neil Schlager]
       p. cm.
Includes bibliographical references and indexes.
Contents: v. 1. A-J
Summary: Emphasizes current technology in providing information on the invention, manufacturing, and future uses of thirty common high-interest products.
      ISBN 0-7876-0870-X (set)
1. Manufactures—Juvenile literature.   [1. Manufactures.]
I. Lim, Kyung-Sun. II. Schlager, Neil, 1966- . III. Title.
TS146.W57   1996
670—dc20
                                                  96-12523
                                                       CIP
                                                        AC

♾™This book is printed on acid-free paper that meets the minimum requirements of American National Standard for Information Sciences—-Permanence Paper for Printed Library Materials, ANSI Z39.48-1984.

ISBN 0-7876-0870-X (set); ISBN 0-7876-0871-8 (volume 1); ISBN 0-7876-0872-6 (volume 2)

Printed in the United States of America

10 9 8 7 6 5 4 3 2 1

Contents

Reader's Guide

CDs, Super Glue, and Salsa: How Everyday Products Are Made, Series 2, answers all the questions about 30 products students use, see, hear about, or read about every day. From common items like pencils and smoke detectors, to the less-common, like bungee cords and player pianos, entries describe in vivid detail the whys and hows of the inventions, provide step-by-step descriptions of the manufacturing processes, and even offer predictions about product enhancements for the future.

CDs, Super Glue, and Salsa's photos, illustrations, and lively, fun-to-read language make it easy to understand the sometimes complicated processes involved in creating these everyday products. Use Series 2 along with Series 1 for a one-stop guide to the details behind 60 of today's most fascinating products.

Format

CDs, Super Glue, and Salsa entries are arranged alphabetically across two volumes. In each entry, students will learn the secrets behind the manufacture of a product through the details of its history, including who invented it and why; how it was developed and how it works; how and from what it is made; how the product might be used in the future; information on factory tours and museums where students can learn more; and a list of other references that offer additional information.

Entry subheads make it easy for students to scan entries for just the information they need at a glance. Entries include sections that feature the following information:

- Background of product, including history or development
- Raw materials needed for production
- Design of product and how it works
- Manufacturing process
- Quality control

- Byproducts
- Future products
- Where to learn more

Additonal Features

The many boxed sections and call-outs present entertaining and interesting facts that students can use to jazz up reports and projects. The uses and manufacturing processes of each product are enlivened with 110 photos and 69 illustrations. Each volume includes a general subject index, including entries from Series 1, that provides easy access to entries by listing important terms, processes, materials, and people.

Comments and Suggestions

We welcome comments on this work as well as suggestions for other products to be featured in future editions of *CDs, Super Glue, and Salsa.* Please write: Editor, *CDs, Super Glue, and Salsa,* U·X·L, 835 Penobscot Bldg., Detroit, Michigan 48226-4094; call toll-free: 1-800-877-4253; or fax toll-free: 1-800-414-5043.

Photo Credits

Photographs appearing in *CDs, Super Glue, and Salsa: How Everyday Products Are Made,* Series 2, were received from the following sources:

Courtesy of Allied Signal Safety Restraint Systems: pp. 1, 7, 8; AP/Wide World Photos: pp. 2, 55, 75, 76, 125, 129, 179, 214, 246, 279, 280, 281, 287, 288; Field Mark Publications. Reproduced with permission: pp. 11, 37, 39, 40, 48, 57, 62, 64, 74, 83, 96, 97, 98, 111, 161, 164, 169, 172, 178, 183, 185, 186, 188, 192, 193, 194, 199, 213, 217, 234, 235, 241, 245, 248, 250, 256, 261, 264, 268, 271, 273, 276; © Chromosohm/Sohm 1987/The Stock Market: p. 12; Courtesy of Scimed Life Systems: p. 17; Courtesy of Rawlings Sporting Goods: pp. 18, 19, 24; © Ariel Skelley/The Stock Market: p. 25; Courtesy of Motorola: pp. 26, 27, 33, 34; Courtesy of Trek Bicycle Corp.: pp. 36, 43; Archive Photos/London Daily Express: p. 49; Courtesy of the Wm. Wrigley Jr. Company: p. 58; Courtesy of Bausch & Lomb, Inc.: pp. 66, 67, 72; Courtesy of Fireworks by Grucci. Used with permission: pp. 86, 88, 94; © 1992 William Whitehurst/The Stock Market: p. 93; Courtesy of New Holland North America, Inc.: pp. 102, 103, 105; © 1995 Mike Chew/The Stock Market: p. 113; © Paul Barton 1993/The Stock Market: p. 117; Courtesy of Kawasaki Robotics (USA), Inc.: p. 119; From the Collection of Henry Ford Museum & Greenfield Village. Used with permission: pp. 120, 162, 265; Archive Photos: p. 122; © Chris Sorensen/The Stock Market: p. 131; Allied Signal Corporation. Used with permission: pp. 133, 140; © 1991 Joe Towers Com./The Stock Market: p. 135; © 1992 Tom Ives/The Stock Market: p. 170; Reprinted by permission of Eastman Kodak Company: pp. 202, 203, 204, 206; Courtesy of Story & Clark Pianos: pp. 219, 223; Courtesy of Keener Rubber Company: pp. 225, 230, 231; Courtesy of First Alert Marketing: pp. 233, 239; Photograph © David Young-Wolff. Photo Edit: p. 255; Photograph by Michelle Bridwell. Photo Edit: p. 257; Photograph by Michael Newman. Photo Edit: p. 262; © 1984 Peter Angelo Simon/The Stock Market: p. 267.

Ketchup

Ketchup, a tangy, seasoned tomato sauce, is one of America's favorite condiments (something used to enhance the flavor of food). Although most people use ketchup, also spelled catsup, as a topping for hamburgers, hot dogs, french fries, and eggs, it is also an ingredient in sauces, dressings, baked beans, and stews. During the mid-1990s the sales of ketchup exceeded $400 million annually.

Early Ketchup

Ketchup originated in ancient China as a brine of pickled fish or shellfish called "ke-tsiap." Neighboring countries adapted their own variations of ketchup using fish brine, herbs, and spices. In the late 1600s, English sailors visiting Malaysia and Singapore were so impressed with the sauce that they took samples home. English cooks tried to duplicate the spicy sauce, but they did not have some of the exotic Asian ingredients. As substitutes, they added cucumbers, mushrooms, nuts, or oysters.

Ketchup originated in ancient China as a brine of pickled fish or shellfish called "ke-tsiap."

Today's Ketchup

In the late 1700s, New Englanders created a ketchup that is close to what is on today's grocery shelves. When Maine seamen returned from Mexico and the Spanish West Indies with seeds of an exotic New World fruit called tomato, ketchup quickly became a popular sauce for codfish cakes, meat, and other foods.

Making ketchup at home was hard, time-consuming work. The tomato mixture, cooked in heavy iron kettles on wood-burning stoves, required constant stirring to prevent it from burning. Cleaning the pre-

By the 1920s, when this photo was taken, ketchup operations were highly mechanized.

Ketchup is also spelled catsup because people used to feed the sauce to their cats during the 1700s—it was something that "a cat sups on."

serving kettles was no easy task, either. To the relief of many homemakers, ketchup became commercially available in the latter part of the 1800s. The Pittsburgh-based H. J. Heinz Company developed one of the first brands of mass-marketed ketchup.

Packaging

The classic glass, narrow-neck design of the Heinz ketchup bottle established a standard for the industry. The narrow-neck bottle simplified pouring the ketchup and minimized oxidation (a chemical reaction that occurs when a substance is mixed with oxygen), which could darken the sauce. Glass was an ideal container because it did not react with the ketchup and allowed the consumer to see the product. Initially, the glass bottles were sealed with cork dipped by hand into wax to prevent air from getting inside, then topped with foil to further protect the sauce from contamination. By the turn of the century, screw caps provided a more convenient closure.

In the 1980s plastic squeezable containers revolutionized ketchup packaging and soon outsold glass containers. Plastic was not only more convenient than glass for pouring the thick sauce, but also safer because it didn't shatter. In response to environmental concerns, plastic containers were later made recyclable.

Ketchup Materials

The main ingredients of ketchup are tomatoes, sweeteners, white vinegar, salt, spices, flavorings, onion, and/or garlic. The sweeteners are usually granulated (formed into grains) cane sugar or beet sugar. Other sweeteners include dextrose or liquid sugar in the form of corn or glucose syrup. The vinegar helps to preserve the ketchup. The spices commonly used to enhance the flavor of the tomatoes are allspice, cassia, cinnamon, cayenne, cloves, pepper, ginger, mustard, and paprika. Some manufacturers believe that whole spices produce a superior, more mild flavor than ground spices or spice oils. More modern processes use premixed or encapsulated (enclosed in a capsule) spices, which are easier to use but more expensive. Whatever the form, the spices must be of a high quality for better flavor.

Brands of ketchup have slightly different formulas, which vary primarily in the amounts of spices or flavorings. Thicker consistencies require more sugar and spices relative to the amount of tomato juice. Formulas must occasionally be adjusted because of variations in the fruit's acid and sugar content, which occur because of changes in growing conditions and types of tomatoes.

FOOD FOR THOUGHT

- *97 percent of American households use ketchup.*
- *Americans consume an average of 3 bottles of ketchup annually.*
- *A tablespoon of ketchup contains only 16 calories and no fat.*
- *4 tablespoons of ketchup are the nutritional equivalent of a medium-sized tomato.*

The introduction of plastic squeezable containers in the 1980s dramatically reduced the frustration of pouring thick ketchup.

The Manufacturing Process

Preparing tomatoes

1 Tomatoes are harvested mechanically during June and July. The fruit usually is transferred by water from the trucks into a flume, or inclined channel. The water method washes the tomatoes and protects them from bruising while they pass from the truck to the factory. The U.S. Department of Agriculture or state inspectors approve and grade, or rate, tomatoes to meet initial requirements. The tomatoes are sorted, washed, and chopped. Next, precooking in stainless steel vats preserves the tomatoes and destroys bacteria (see fig. 41).

Plastic squeeze bottles make pouring ketchup easier. People use ketchup as a flavor enhancer for many types of foods, including eggs.

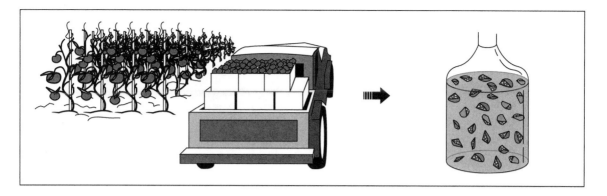

Fig. 41. Tomatoes are harvested and taken to the factory by truck. They are washed and chopped, then precooked in a stainless steel vat.

Pulping

2 The chopped and precooked tomatoes are pumped into pulping machines, or cyclones, which separate seeds, skins, and stems from the pulp (see fig. 42). The pulp and juice are filtered through screens and processed further into ketchup, though some may be stored in a paste for ketchup processing at a later date.

Adding ingredients and cooking

3 The pulp is pumped into cooking tanks or kettles and heated to boiling. Precise amounts of sweeteners, vinegar, salt, spices, and flavorings are added to the tomato pulp (see fig. 42). Most spices are added early in the cooking process. To avoid excessive evaporation, spice oils and vinegar are mixed in later. Onions and garlic can be mixed in with the spices, placed in a separate bag, or chopped and added to the pulp. Salt and sugar may be added at any stage of cooking. The mixture cooks for 30 to 45 minutes and is stirred by rotating blades installed in the cookers. The temperature must be carefully regulated to ensure absorption of the ingredients without overcooking, which creates a flat body.

Finishing

4 Once cooking is complete, the ketchup mixture passes through a finishing machine. Finishers remove excess fiber and particles through screens, creating a creamy consistency. The ketchup then passes to a holding tank.

Ketchup manufacturers look for tomatoes that are superior in color, flavor, and texture; slight variations in tomatoes can alter the flavor and color of the finished product.

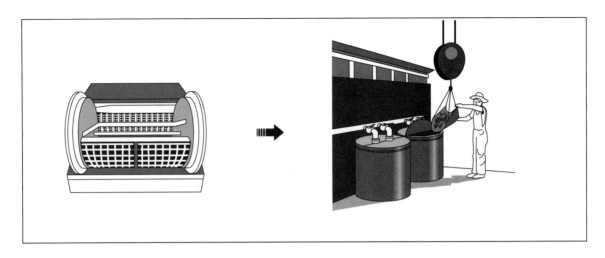

Fig. 42. Pulping machines separate the seed, skins, and pulp of the tomatoes. The pulp is then placed in cooking tanks where sweeteners and spices are added.

The entire process of ketchup manufacturing— from the time the tomatoes arrive at the plant, to the sealing of the containers— generally takes two to three hours.

5 The ketchup may be processed further at higher temperatures and pressures to achieve an even smoother consistency.

Removing air

6 The ketchup must be de-aerated (to remove oxygen) to prevent discoloration and growth of bacteria (see fig. 43). Excess air may also create unattractive air pockets in the ketchup and interfere with the process of closing the containers.

Filling

7 To prevent contamination, the ketchup passes from receiving tanks to the filling machines at a temperature not lower than 190 degrees Fahrenheit (88 degrees Celsius). The containers are filled with ketchup and immediately sealed to keep the product fresh (see fig. 43). Ketchup containers come in various sizes and shapes, including 14-ounce bottles, Number 10 cans, pouch packs, room-service sizes, and single-serve packets.

Cooling

8 The containers must be cooled to prevent flavor loss, which can occur when ketchup stays at high temperatures after cooking is complete. Containers of ketchup may be cooled in cold air or cold water.

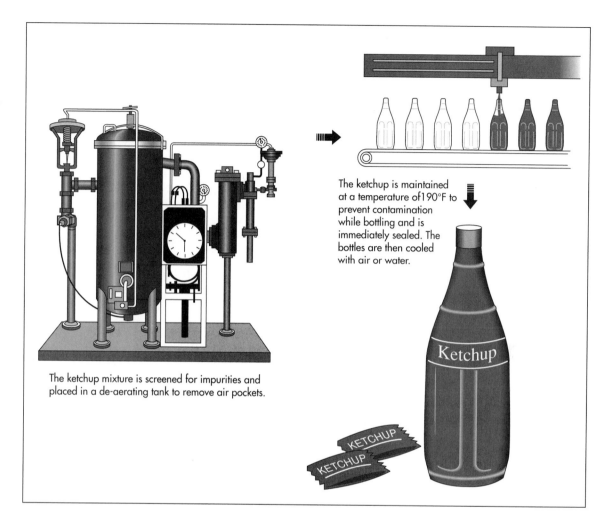

The ketchup is maintained at a temperature of 190°F to prevent contamination while bottling and is immediately sealed. The bottles are then cooled with air or water.

The ketchup mixture is screened for impurities and placed in a de-aerating tank to remove air pockets.

Fig. 43. Preparing ketchup for bottling.

Labeling and packing

9 Finally, the ketchup containers are labeled and coded with product information, including ingredients, date and location of manufacture, and shelf life (how long the ketchup remains fresh after packaging). The bottled ketchup may be inspected again before shipping.

Some ketchups contain as much as 25 to 30 percent sugar.

Quality Control

To ensure quality during the manufacturing process, samples of the product are taken at various stages by workers. The tomatoes, other ingredi-

KETCHUP CODING

To find out when a bottle of Heinz's ketchup was bottled, look for the four-digit number on the cap (ignoring the first two letters) of the container. The first three digits indicate the day of bottling, and the last digit indicates the year. For example, if the number on the cap is 1105, 110 would mean the 110th day of the year and 5 would mean the year 1995.

Ketchup containers come in various sizes and shapes, including 14-ounce bottles, Number 10 cans, pouch packs, room-service sizes, and single-serve packets.

ents, and all of the processing equipment that comes into contact with the product are inspected routinely. To guarantee quality after the product has been purchased, manufacturers recommend that once a container is opened, it should be refrigerated to avoid a change in color, flavor, and consistency.

Future Ketchup

Ketchup manufacturers continue to improve the quality of ketchup by developing tomato strains that are superior in color, flavor, and firmness. Tomato hybrids (a new type of tomato produced by pairing different varieties of tomatoes) are also developed to improve resistance to disease and rot, thus decreasing the need for pesticides.

During the 1990s, in response to consumer demand for more healthful foods, ketchup manufacturers created low-calorie, low-salt ketchup alternatives. The increasing popularity of **salsa**s (see entry in Series I) and marinades also influenced manufacturers to develop salsa-style ketchups that were lower in sugar content. Packaging technology continues to improve as consumers demand safer, more convenient, and recyclable containers.

WHERE TO LEARN MORE

Coyle, L. Patrick Jr. *The World Encyclopedia of Food*. Facts on File, 1982, p. 338.

Gould, Wilbur A. *Tomato Production, Processing, and Quality Evaluation*. Second ed. AVI Publishing Company, Inc., 1983.

Steingarten, Jeffrey. "Simply Red," *Vogue*. August 1992, pp. 244, 298-300.

Neon Sign

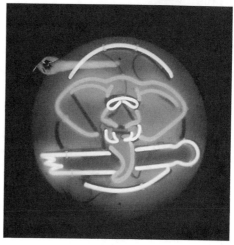

A neon sign is a lighting display made of glass tubes that have been filled with a gas and bent into the shape of letters or decorative designs. When a high-voltage electrical current is passed through the gas, the tubes emit (release) light. Although neon gas was originally used in these signs, several other gases are also used. These gases, along with different tints and phosphor (a substance that emits light after absorbing radiation) coatings for the glass tubes, produce a spectrum of more than 50 brilliant colors.

Neon signs can be as simple as a small advertising sign for soda, or as complex as a multistory facade on a Las Vegas casino.

Early Neon Signs

Neon signs evolved from scientific experiments in which various gases were subjected to high-voltage currents. In 1856, German inventor Johann Heinrich Wilhelm Geissler (1815-79) produced a light source by passing a high-voltage alternating current through a low-pressure gas sealed in a glass tube. Later experiments showed that almost all gases would conduct an electric current, and that many would produce light. The problem was that the light produced by most of the common gases, like carbon dioxide, quickly sputtered and died.

In 1898, while developing a method for the fractional distillation (separating a mixture of liquids that boil at different temperatures) of liquid air (a cold liquid formed when air is put under great pressure and cooled), British chemists Sir William Ramsay (1852-1916) and Morris William Travers (1872-1961) discovered the rare gas elements neon, argon, krypton, and xenon. Using these gases in sealed glass tubes, they produced col-

Downtown Las Vegas at night. The whole city is illuminated by neon and other lights.

Neon and other gases, along with different tints and phosphor coatings for the glass tubes, produce a spectrum of more than 50 brilliant colors.

ored light sources that didn't die right away, ranging from a bright red-dish-orange for neon to an intense grayish-blue or violet for argon.

Fractional distillation of liquid air remained an expensive process until 1907 when chemists Georges Claude (1870-1960) of France and Carl Paul Gottfried von Linde (1842-1934) of Germany developed a more economical method. Claude's original interest was to produce quantities of oxygen for hospitals and industries. Realizing that the other gases (neon, argon, krypton, xenon) produced by this distillation process had no ready market, Claude looked for potential applications. After utilizing the previous experimental work of Ramsay and Travers, he began promoting illuminated signs using tubes filled with neon gas. He displayed his first neon sign at an exposition in Paris in 1910, and made his first commercial installation in 1912. By 1915, business was so promising that he formed the Claude Neon sign company and began selling franchises.

Neon signs came to the United States in 1923 when a Los Angeles car dealer, Earle C. Anthony, bought two of Claude's signs for his Packard dealership. Throughout the 1920s and 1930s, neon tubes were used for signs as well as decorative displays, and they became an integral part of the architecture of many buildings. By 1947 several casinos in Las Vegas began to draw attention with their elaborate neon lights.

Today's Neon Signs

During the 1950s and 1960s, neon signs were slowly displaced by plastic signs illuminated from the inside with fluorescent tubes. Recently, neon has made a comeback in commercial signs and as an artistic medium. It's also starting to show up in the home. Neon clocks, lamps, mirrors, phones, and poster frames are becoming very popular. These items come in a rainbow of colors, fit with almost any decor, and literally brighten up a room.

Design

With only a few exceptions, each neon sign is unique. It must be designed to fit the desired display within a certain amount of available space. The width of the tubing, how far the tubing can be bent, and the overall length of tubing that can be powered by the transformer (the device used to transfer electrical energy from one circuit to another) can determine the final design. For example, the narrower the tube, the brighter the light. At the same time, narrow tubing requires more power, thus limiting the amount of tubing one transformer can handle.

Neon Sign Materials

Although neon gas was originally used in all neon signs, it is now used only to produce reds and oranges. Argon, or an argon-neon mixture, is used in most signs today. To increase the strength of the light, a small amount of mercury is added to the argon, creating an intense blue. This light strikes a variety of light-emitting phosphorescent materials coated on the inside of the glass tube to produce various colors. Optical tints in various colors may also be used, or the glass may be left clear if a strong blue light is desired. Xenon, krypton, and helium gases are sometimes used for special color effects.

The glass tubing used in neon signs is made from soft lead glass that is easily bent and formed. It ranges from 0.3 to 1 inch (8 to 25 millimeters) in

Although neon gas was originally used in all neon signs, it is now used only to produce reds and oranges. Argon, or an argon-neon mixture, is used in most signs.

diameter and comes in lengths of 4-5 feet (1.2 to 1.5 meters). The electrodes (conductors) in each end of a section of illuminated tubing are usually very pure iron surrounded by a tubular glass jacket or envelope with one end open. A wire is attached to the electrode and passes through the closed end of the glass envelope. The closed end is sealed into the end of the sign tubing with the open end protruding into the tube.

The high-voltage electricity to power the sign is provided by a transformer that converts the 120 volts from the electrical lines to as much as 15,000 volts for the sign. The transformers are connected to the electrodes in the sign using special wire, called GTO wire, that is insulated. This wire is also used to connect the individual sections of illuminated tubing. The wire is attached to the transformer through an insulated housing made of a specialized glass (borosilicate glass) with a spring connection on one end. The transformer and wires are purchased from a separate manufacturer and installed by the sign maker.

This neon sign in New York City's Chinatown is an example of the small, indoor signs supported by a thin, almost invisible, framework.

Tubes that are to be filled with neon to form a red or orange light and argon to form a blue light are not tinted.

The sign tubing is supported in several ways. Small indoor signs usually have a thin steel skeleton framework that supports both the tubing and the power transformer. The framework is painted black so it will be less visible, making the sign seem to float in space. Large outdoor signs may be supported by wood, steel, or aluminum structures. The glass tubing is held by glass supports with metal bases. The transformer is placed inside a cabinet to protect it from the weather.

The Manufacturing Process

Manufacturing neon signs is largely a manual process. It consists of bend-

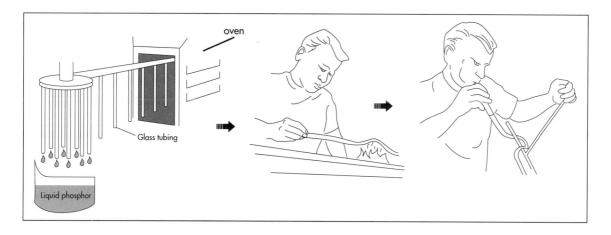

Fig. 44. Glass tubing is cleaned and placed vertically in a coating machine. Liquid phosphor suspension is forced into the tube and then drained out. Next, the glass tubing is heated using a variety of burners, and bent by hand. To prevent the softened tube from collapsing, the tube bender gently blows air into a blow hose.

ing the tubing and attaching the electrodes, removing any impurities from within the tubing, then removing the air and adding the gas.

Preparing the tubing

1 Glass tubing is cleaned and placed vertically in a coating machine, which blows a liquid phosphor into the tube (see fig. 44). The tubes are placed vertically in an oven that dries the coating. If color tints are used, they are applied in a similar manner.

Bending the tubing

2 The design of the sign is laid out in full size on a heat-resistant sheet of asbestos. The glass tubing is carefully heated and softened using a variety of burners (see fig. 44). Gas-fired ribbon burners are used to make curves in round letters and the sweeping curves of script. Smaller hand torches are used to heat shorter lengths. Using the asbestos template as a guide, the tubing is bent by hand. The tube benders do not wear gloves because they must be able to feel when the glass is warm and soft enough to make the bend. To prevent the softened tubing from collapsing, the tube bender attaches a short length of flexible hose, called a blow hose, to one end. While the glass is still soft, the tube bender gently blows into the hose to force the tubing back to its original diameter (see fig. 44). Misshapen tubes will not operate properly.

Once chiefly used in business establishments, neon displays have found their way into consumer products such as telephones and automobile license plate frames.

Manufacturing neon signs is largely a manual process. It consists of bending the tubing and attaching the electrodes, removing any impurities from within the tubing, then removing the air and adding the gas.

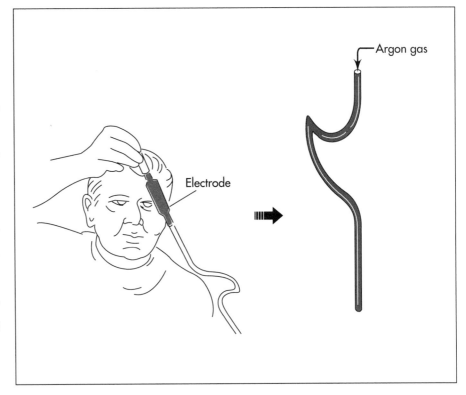

Fig. 45. The shape of the letter or design is formed, and an electrode is fused onto each end. Eventually the gas is inserted.

3 Large neon signs usually are made of several sections of glass tubing about 8 to 10 feet (2.4 to 3.1 meters) long. To make each section, the ends of two lengths of tubing are heated and spliced together. When the shape of the lettering or design has been formed for a section, an electrode is heated and fused onto each end. A small piece, called a tubulation port, is added to allow a vacuum pump to remove air from the tube. This tubulation port may be part of one of the electrodes or may be a separate piece joined into the tubing.

Bombarding the tubing

4 A process known as bombarding is used to remove any impurities from the glass, phosphors, and electrodes. First the air inside the tubing is removed. After the vacuum reaches a certain level, dry air is allowed back in until it reaches a certain amount of the pressure. The longer the tubing, the lower the pressure may have to be. Then a very

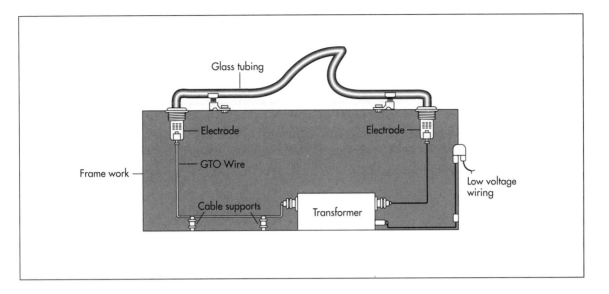

Fig. 46. The neon sign is then attached to a transformer and mounted inside a framework to protect the wiring and elements from the weather.

high-current transformer is connected to the electrodes. The high current heats the glass to about 420 degrees Fahrenheit (216 degrees Celsius), and the metal electrode is heated to about 1400 degrees Fahrenheit (760 degrees Celsius). This heating forces the impurities out of the materials, and the vacuum pump carries the impurities out of the system.

Filling the tube

5 Once the tube has cooled, the gas is inserted under a low pressure (see fig. 45). The gas must be free from impurities in order for the sign to operate properly and have a long life. Once the tube is filled, the tubulation port is heated and sealed off.

Aging the tube

6 The finished gas-filled tubing is put through an aging process. Sometimes this process is referred to as "burning in the tube." The purpose is to allow the gas in the tube to stabilize and operate properly. A transformer, often rated slightly higher than the normal operating current, is attached to the electrodes. The tube should come to full illumination within 15 minutes if neon is used. It may take up to a few hours for argon. If a small amount of mercury is to be added to an argon tube, a droplet is placed into the tubulation port before it is sealed. The droplet is

Any problem such as a flicker in the gas or a hot spot on the tube indicates the tubing must be opened and the bombarding and filling processes repeated.

A NEW COMPETITOR

*A new competitor to neon lighting may be fiber optics (see **optical fiber** entry in Series I). Side-emitting fiber-optic systems (glass or plastic fibers that emit light, sent from a central light source, out their sides) are able to produce the same effects as neon lighting at lower installation, energy, and maintenance costs. And if that's not enough, with fiber optics there's no gas fill to leak out, the colors can be changed easily, no electric current is emitted, and the bundled strands are safer to apply in outdoor areas, such as fountain illumination, than neon lighting. Even though there are some limitations—the fibers cannot be bent as far as neon tubing and they (especially plastic fibers) absorb blue light, giving the colors a more subdued look—fiber-optic lighting is surging ahead in the lighting industry.*

A well-built neon sign should have a life of more than 30,000 hours. As a comparison, the average 100-watt light bulb has a rated life of 750 to 1,000 hours.

then rolled from one end to the other to coat the electrodes after the aging process. Any problem such as a flicker in the gas or a hot spot on the tube indicates the tubing must be opened and the bombarding and filling processes repeated.

Installation and mounting

7 Small neon signs are mounted on their framework and wired in the shop (see fig. 46). Larger signs may be mounted in pieces and put into place on the building or other support structure where they are interconnected and wired. Very large installations may require months to complete.

Quality Control

Pure materials and careful manufacturing processes are required to produce a properly operating neon sign. A well-built neon sign should have a life of more than 30,000 hours. As a comparison, the average 100-watt **light bulb** (see also entry in Series I) has a rated life of 750 to 1,000 hours.

To meet the requirements of the Underwriters Laboratories (UL) and obtain a UL listing, neon signs require a series of tests by independent testing agencies. Neon signs must also meet the requirements of the National Electrical Code. Outdoor signs must comply with local building codes in their construction and electrical wiring.

Future Neon Signs

Recent developments in neon sign design include small, electronic transformers that make the hum of older neon signs a thing of the past. Neon signs that blink or appear to move are now controlled by programmable electronic controls that have replaced electromechanical cam-and-switch controls. No longer only used in business, neon displays have also found their way into consumer products such as telephones and automobile license plate frames. There are even neon displays that cover portions of the exterior of cars for the ultimate in a "flashy" vehicle.

Neon signs are expected to continue to enjoy a resurgence of interest and applications. Some Japanese companies have expanded the palette of neon lights far beyond the 50 or so colors now commonly used. Neon displays that appear to move are also getting more complex and flamboyant with the aid of computer controls.

WHERE TO LEARN MORE

Gromer, Cliff. "Neon Cowboy: Computer Magic Makes Vegas Lights Come to Life," *Popular Mechanics*. September 1994, pp. 56-57.

Miller, Samuel C. *Neon Techniques and Handling: Handbook of Neon Sign and Cold Cathode Lighting*. ST Publications, 1985.

Resnick, Rosalind. "Hot Lights on Wheels," *Nation's Business*. June 1994, pp. 14-15.

Stern, Rudi. *Let There Be Neon*. Harry N. Abrams, Inc., 1979.

Woods, Wilton. "Neon Comes Home," *Fortune*. March 20, 1995, p. 22.

Peanut Butter

People in the United States eat 800,000 pounds of peanut butter each year, making peanut butter the country's most popular food.

Peanuts

Peanuts, which are actually legumes (plants having pods that contain seeds) and not nuts, originated in South America. It is believed that they were first brought to Europe by Spanish explorers and then traded for elephant tusks and spices in Africa. Later, peanuts were introduced to North America from Africa, but were not considered a staple crop until the 1890s. At that time they were promoted as a replacement for the cotton crop destroyed by the boll weevil (a long-snouted beetle). Although there are a few varieties of peanuts, it is mostly the smaller, runner-type peanuts, grown in Alabama, Florida, and Georgia, that are used to make peanut butter.

Early Peanut Butter

Peanut butter originated in Haiti around the end of the seventeenth century. Haitians used a wood mortar and a pestle with a metal cap to pound the peanuts into a paste. During the nineteenth century in the United States, shelled (shell removed), roasted peanuts were chopped or pounded into a creamy paste in a cloth bag. A physician in St. Louis, Missouri, started manufacturing peanut butter commercially in 1890. Featured at the St. Louis World's Fair as a health food, peanut butter was recommended for infants and invalids because of its high nutritional value. Around 1915 American botanist and inventor George Washington Carver started experimenting with peanuts. He eventually produced 300 products out of peanuts, including peanut butter.

Farmers began investing in this new cash crop when they realized that the financial rewards from pig feed were beginning to dwindle. Thus,

GEORGE WASHINGTON CARVER (1864?-1943)

Throughout his career, American botanist and educator George Washington Carver searched for ways to make small Southern family farms, often African-American owned, more self-sufficient. He also wanted to wean farmers away from the annual production of soil-depleting staple crops like cotton and tobacco. The only way he could achieve these goals, however, was to increase the demand for peanuts. He eventually succeeded by inventing new or popularizing existing peanut products including peanut butter, milk, makeup, paint, shampoo, ink, shaving cream, and ice cream.

with increased mechanized cultivation and harvesting, the availability of peanuts grew as did the development and production of peanut butter. Most recently, peanut butter has been used primarily as a sandwich spread, although it also appears in prepared dishes and confections.

Peanut Butter Ingredients

The peanut, rich in fat, protein, vitamin B, phosphorus, and iron, has significant food value. In its final ground form, peanut butter consists of about 90 to 95 percent carefully selected, blanched, dry-roasted peanuts. To improve smoothness, spreadability and flavor, other ingredients are added, including salt (1.5 percent), hydrogenated vegetable oil (0.125 percent), dextrose (2 percent), and corn syrup or honey (2 to 4 percent). To enhance peanut butter's nutritive value, ascorbic acid and yeast are also added. The amounts of other ingredients can vary as long as they are not more than 10 percent of the peanut butter. Peanut butter contains 50 to 52 percent fat, 28 to 29 percent protein, 2 to 5 percent carbohydrate, and 1 to 2 percent water.

In its definition of peanut butter, the U.S. Food and Drug Administration (FDA) stipulates that seasoning and stabilizing ingredients must not "exceed 10 percent of the weight of the finished food." Furthermore, the

Around 1925, peanut butter was sold from an open tub, with half an inch of oil on the surface. Although the paste was sticky and made people very thirsty after eating it, they liked it.

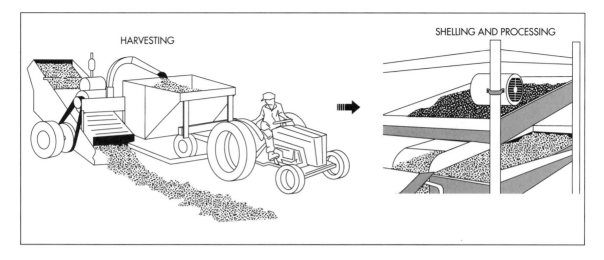

Fig. 47. After harvesting, the peanuts are cleaned, shelled, and graded for size.

FDA states that "artificial flavorings, artificial sweeteners, chemical preservatives, added vitamins, and color additives are not suitable ingredients of peanut butter." A product that does not conform to the FDA's standards must be labeled "imitation peanut butter."

The Manufacturing Process

Planting and harvesting peanuts

1 Peanuts (or seeds) are planted in April or May, depending upon the climate. Soon a plant emerges followed by a yellow flower. After blooming and then wilting, the flower bends to the ground, enters the soil, then grows underground. From late August through October, the peanuts are removed from vines by portable, mechanical pickers (see fig. 47).

2 Peanuts from the pickers are delivered to warehouses, cleaned, and stored unshelled in silos or warehouses.

Shelling and processing

3 Shelling consists of removing the shell (or hull) of peanuts using a series of rollers (see fig. 47). The shelled peanuts are then graded for size color, defects, spots, and broken skins.

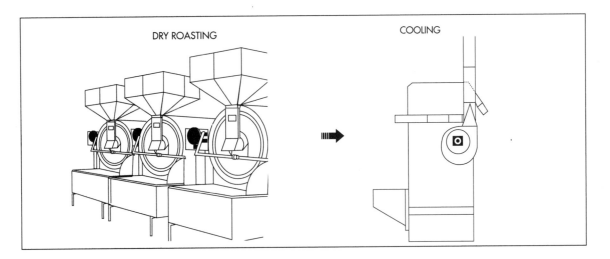

DRY ROASTING

COOLING

Fig. 48. Next, the peanuts are dry roasted in large ovens, and then they are transferred to cooling machines, where suction fans draw cooling air over the peanuts.

4 Finally, the peanuts are shipped in large bulk containers or sacks to peanut butter manufacturers. If edible peanuts need to be stored for more than 60 days, they are placed in refrigerated storage, where they may be held for as long as 25 months.

Dry roasting and cooling

5 Peanut butter manufacturers first dry roast the peanuts, using either the batch or continuous method. Some manufacturers prefer the continuous method (roasting a variety of peanuts together at one time), while others prefer the batch method (roasting peanuts according to type, size, moisture content, etc.). This entry will focus on the batch method of dry roasting peanuts.

In the batch method, peanuts are roasted in 400-pound lots in a revolving oven. The peanuts are heated at 320 degrees Fahrenheit (160 degrees Celsius) and held at this temperature until they are done (see fig. 48). A photometer indicates when the cooking is complete.

6 To quickly stop the peanuts from cooking and to produce a uniform product, the hot peanuts pass from the roaster directly to a blower-cooler vat (see fig. 48). A large volume of cool air reduces the temperature of the peanuts to 86 degrees Fahrenheit (30 degrees Celsius). Once cooled, the peanuts pass through a gravity separator that removes foreign material, such as pieces of shell, stones, or twigs.

The world's largest peanut butter and jelly sandwich, made at the Penta Hotel in Atlanta, Georgia, in 1992, weighed 2,500 pounds!

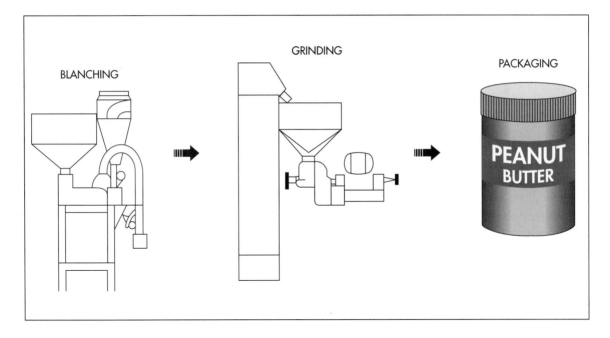

BLANCHING

GRINDING

PACKAGING

PEANUT BUTTER

Fig. 49. After blanching—removal of the skins by heat or water—the peanuts are pulverized and ground with salt, dextrose, and hydrogenated oil stabilizer in a grinding machine. Once cooled, the peanut butter is ready to be packaged.

Adding hydrogenated vegetable oil to peanut butter smooths its texture and keeps the peanut oil from separating.

Blanching

7 The skins (or seed coats) are now removed with either heat or water. In heat blanching, the peanuts are exposed to a temperature of 280 degrees Fahrenheit (137.7 degrees Celsius) for up to 20 minutes to loosen and crack the skins (see fig. 49). After cooling, the peanuts are passed through the blancher in a continuous stream and subjected to a thorough but gentle rubbing between brushes or ribbed rubber belting. The skins are rubbed off and blown into porous bags.

In water blanching, the peanuts are arranged in troughs (shallow receptacles), then rolled between sharp, stationary (nonmoving) blades to slit the skins on opposite sides. The skins are removed as a spiral conveyor carries the peanuts through a one-minute scalding water bath and then under an oscillating (moving back and forth) canvas-covered pad, which rubs off their skins. The blanched kernels are then dried for at least six hours by a flow of air set at 120 degrees Fahrenheit (48.8 degrees Celsius).

8 The blanched nuts are mechanically screened and inspected on a conveyor belt to remove scorched and rotten nuts or other undesirable matter. A high-speed electric color sorter removes discolored nuts.

Peanut butter and jelly sandwiches rate among the most popular lunches with American children.

Grinding

9 Peanut butter is usually made by two grinding operations. The first reduces the nuts to a medium grind and the second creates a fine, smooth texture (see fig. 49). To make chunky peanut butter, either the peanuts are ground to a chunky consistency or peanut pieces are mixed with regular peanut butter.

At the same time the peanuts are fed into the grinder, about 2 percent salt, dextrose, and hydrogenated oil stabilizer are added and thoroughly dispersed into the ground nut mixture.

10 Peanuts are kept under constant pressure from the start to the finish of the grinding process to assure uniform grinding and to protect the product from air bubbles. A heavy screw feeds the peanuts into the grinder. From the grinder, the peanut butter goes into a stainless steel hopper (a funnel-shaped container) where it is cooled from 170 to 120 degrees Fahrenheit (76.6 to 48.8 degrees Celsius) before it is packaged.

Each shipment of peanuts that arrives at the peanut factory is tested for Aflatoxin—a poisonous substance caused by mold in peanuts.

The shelf life of an unopened jar of peanut butter is about 6 months. An opened jar stored in the cupboard lasts about 2 to 3 months, around 4 months if it is refrigerated.

Packaging

11 The cooled peanut butter is mechanically packed into jars, capped, and labeled. Since proper packaging is the main factor in reducing spoilage, manufacturers use vacuum packing to seal out oxygen. Finally, the jars are packed into cartons and placed in product storage until ready to be shipped out to retail or institutional customers.

Quality Control

Quality control of peanut butter starts on the farm through harvesting and curing (being prepared or preserved by a chemical or physical process), and is then carried through the steps of shelling, storing, and manufacturing the product. In the United States, strict quality control has been maintained on peanuts for many years with cooperation and approval from both the U.S. Department of Agriculture (USDA) and the Food and Drug Administration (FDA). Quality control is handled by the Peanut Administrative Committee, which is an arm of the USDA. Responsibility for raw peanuts rests with the Department of Agriculture. During and after manufacture, quality control is under the supervision of the FDA.

Byproducts

Peanut vines and leaves, which contain a lot of nutrients, are used as fertilizer or to feed livestock. Peanut shells are used mainly as fuel for the boiler generating steam for making electricity that operates the shelling plant. Limited markets exist for peanut shells for roughage in cattle feed, poultry litter, insulation, and filler in artificial fire logs. Potential products include pet litter, a mushroom-growing medium, and floor-sweeping compounds.

Tomorrow's Peanut Butter

In the United States and most of the 53 peanut-producing countries in the world, the production and consumption of peanuts, including peanut butter, is increasing. The quality of peanuts continues to improve to meet higher standards. The convenience peanut butter offers its users and its high nutritional value meet the demands of contemporary lifestyles.

There are many treats one can make with peanut butter, including peanut butter cookies, peanut butter bars, peanut butter coffeecake, peanut butter frosting, and peanut butter milkshakes.

The use of peanuts as food is being introduced to remote parts of the world by American ambassadors, missionaries, and Peace Corps volunteers. Some developing countries, understanding that their food protein scarcity will not be solved through animal proteins alone, are interested in growing the protein-rich peanut crop.

WHERE TO LEARN MORE

Coyle, L. Patrick Jr. *The World Encyclopedia of Food.* Facts on File, 1982, p. 503.

Erlbach, Arlene. *Peanut Butter.* Lerner Publications, 1993.

"The Nuttiest Peanut Butter," *Consumer Reports.* September 1990, p. 588.

"Peanut Butter, It's Not Just for Kids Anymore," *Consumer Reports.* September 1995, p. 576-579.

Woodroof, Jasper Guy, ed. *Peanuts: Production, Processing, Products.* Avi Publishing Company, 1983.

Zisman, Honey. *The Great American Peanut Butter Book: A Book of Recipes, Facts, Figures, and Fun.* St. Martin's Press, 1985.

Pencil

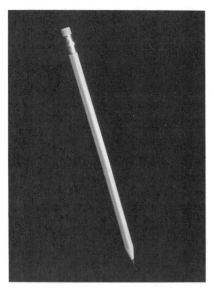

Primitive Pencils

One of the oldest and most widely used writing utensils, the pencil originated in prehistoric times when chalky rocks and charred sticks were used to draw on surfaces as varied as animal hides and cave walls. The Greeks and Romans used flat pieces of lead to draw faint lines on papyrus (a material made from the papyrus plant), but it was not until the late 1400s that the earliest direct ancestor of today's pencil was developed.

The pencil— manufactured at a pace of 6 billion per year in 40 different countries— continues to outsell the ballpoint pen.

Early Graphite Pencils

During the sixteenth century large deposits of graphite, a soft, shiny mineral found in rocks, was discovered near Borrowdale in northwestern England. Because people could not tell the difference between graphite and lead, they referred to graphite as "black lead." It wasn't until 1779 that scientists determined the material they had previously thought was lead was actually a form of microcrystalline carbon (containing small crystals) that they named graphite (from the Greek word *graphein* meaning "to write").

Cut into rods or strips, graphite was heavily wrapped in twine to provide strength and a comfortable handle. The finished product, called a lead pencil, was quite popular. Eventually, a method for gluing strips of wood around graphite was developed in Germany, and the modern pencil began to take shape.

In the late eighteenth century, the Borrowdale mine was depleted, and, as graphite was now less plentiful, other materials had to be mixed with it to create pencils. French chemist Nicolas Jacques Conté discovered that when powdered graphite, powdered clay, and water were mixed, molded, and baked, the finished product wrote as smoothly as pure graphite. Conté also learned that a harder or softer writing core could be produced by varying the proportion of clay and graphite—the more graphite, the blacker and softer the pencil. In 1839, Lothar von Faber of Germany developed a method of making graphite paste into rods of the same thickness. He later invented a machine to cut and groove the pencil wood.

Following the depletion of the once-abundant graphite source at Borrowdale, other graphite mines gradually were established around the world. A number of these mines were set up in the United States, and the first American pencils were manufactured in 1812, after the War of 1812 ended English imports.

Early Patents

William Monroe, a cabinet maker in Concord, Massachusetts, invented a machine that cut and grooved wood slats precisely enough to make pencils. Around that time, American inventor Joseph Dixon developed a method of cutting single cedar cylinders in half, placing the graphite core in one of the halves, and then gluing the two halves back together. The idea of attaching a rubber eraser to a pencil is traced to Hyman W. Lipman, an American whose 1858 U.S. patent was bought by Joseph Rechendorfer in 1872 for a reported $100,000. In 1861, John Eberhard Faber, brother of Lothar von Faber, built the United States' first pencil-making factory in New York City.

Pencil Materials

The most important ingredient in a pencil is the graphite, which most people continue to call lead. Conté's method of combining graphite with clay is still used, and wax or other chemicals are sometimes added as well. Virtually all graphite in pencils today is a manufactured mixture of natural graphite and chemicals.

The wood for pencils must be able to withstand repeated sharpening and cut easily without splintering. Most pencils are made from cedar

WHAT DO THOSE NUMBERS MEAN?

The hardness of a pencil is designated by a number or letter, which is usually imprinted at the top of the pencil. Most manufacturers use the numbers 1 to 4, with 1 being the softest and making the darkest mark. Number 2 pencils (medium-soft) are the ones most commonly used. Pencils sometimes are graded by letters, from 6B, the softest, to 9H, the hardest.

Today's pencils are not made from lead, but from a combination of graphite and clay.

Not all pencils look the same. Some have funny shapes or amusing erasers.

(specifically, California cedar), the choice wood for many years. Cedar has a pleasant odor, does not warp or lose its shape, and is readily available.

Pencil erasers are held on with a ferrule, a metal case that is either glued or fastened on the end of a pencil with metal prongs. The erasers themselves consist of pumice and rubber.

The Manufacturing Process

Now that most commercially used graphite is made in factories rather than mined, manufacturers can easily control its density. The graphite is mixed with clay according to the type of pencil being made—the more graphite used, the softer the pencil and the darker its line. For colored pencils, pigments are added to the clay, and virtually no graphite is used.

Processing the graphite

1 Two methods are used to form the graphite into its finished state. The first is an extrusion method in which the graphite and wax mixture is forced through a narrow hole to create a spaghetti-like string, which is then cut to precise measurements and dried in ovens (see fig. 50).

In the second method, the graphite and clay mixture is poured into a machine called a billet press. A plug is placed over the top of the press, and a metal ram ascends from the bottom to press the mixture into a hard, solid cylinder called a "billet." The billet is then removed from the top of the machine and placed into an extrusion press that forces it through a mold, slicing off strips the size of the pencil core. After being cut to size, the cores pass along a conveyor belt and are collected in a trough to await insertion in the pencil wood.

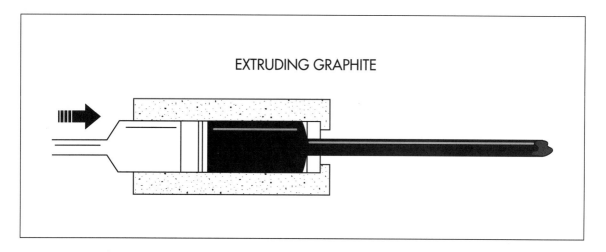

EXTRUDING GRAPHITE

Fig. 50. The first step in pencil manufacturing involves making the graphite core. One method of doing this is through extrusion, in which the graphite mixture is forced through the proper size opening of a die (a tool used to shape solid material).

Making the wood casings

2 The cedar usually arrives at the factory already dried, stained, and waxed, to prevent warping. Logs are then sawed into narrow strips called "slats"; these are about 7.25 inches (18.4 centimeters) long, .25 inch (.635 centimeter) thick, and 2.75 inches (6.98 centimeters) wide (see fig. 51). The slats are placed into a feeder and dropped, one by one, onto a conveyor belt, which moves them along at a constant rate.

3 The slats are then planed (smoothed and leveled) to give them a flat surface. Next, they pass under a cutter head that makes parallel semicircular grooves—one-half as deep as the graphite is thick— along the length of one side of each slat. Continuing along the conveyor belt, half of the slats are coated with a layer of glue, and the cut graphite is laid in the grooves of these slats.

4 The slats without glue—and without graphite in the grooves—are carried on another belt to a machine that picks them up and turns them over, so they are lying on the belt with the grooves facing down. The two conveyor belts then meet, and each unglued slat is placed over a slat with glue and graphite, forming a "sandwich." After the sandwiches are removed from the conveyor belt, they are placed into a metal

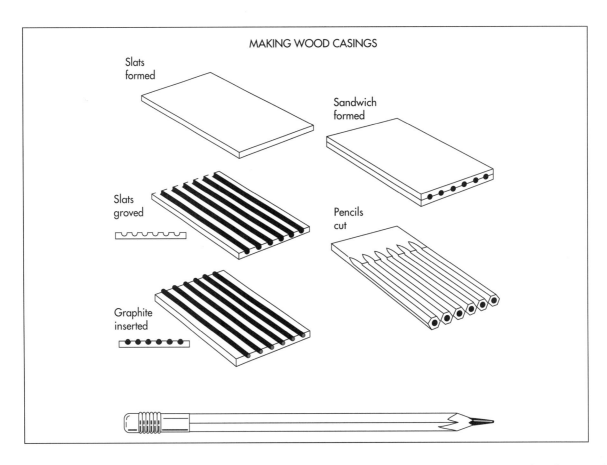

Fig. 51. To make the wood casings for the pencils, square slats are formed, and then grooves are cut into the slats. Next, graphite sticks are inserted into the grooves on one slat, and then a second slat with empty grooves is glued on top of the graphite-filled slat. Correctly sized pencils are cut out of the sandwich, and the eraser and metal ferrule are attached.

The majority of pencils are six-sided, which keeps them from rolling off surfaces.

clamp, squeezed by a hydraulic press, and left clamped together until the glue is dry. Then the pencil ends are trimmed to remove excess glue.

Shaping the pencils

5 The next step is shaping, when the sandwiches actually become pencils. The sandwiches are placed on a conveyor belt and moved through two sets of cutters, one above and one below the belt. The cutters above the sandwiches cut around the top half, while the lower set cuts around the bottom half and separates the finished pencils. The majority of pencils are hexagonal (six-sided), to keep them from rolling off sur-

faces; a single sandwich yields six to nine hexagonal pencils.

Final steps

6 After the pencils have been cut, their surfaces are smoothed by sanders. The pencils are then immersed in a vat of varnish and passed through a felt disk, which removes the excess varnish. After drying, the pencils are put through the process again and again until the desired color is achieved. Finally, the pencils receive a finishing coat.

7 The pencils once again are sent on a conveyor belt through shaping machines, which remove any excess varnish that has accumulated on the ends of the pencils. This step also ensures that all of the pencils are the same length.

8 Erasers are attached, held to the pencil by a round, metal case—the ferrule. First, the ferrule is attached to the pencil, either with glue or with small metal prongs, and then the eraser is inserted and the ferrule clamped around it. In the final step, a heated steel die presses the company logo onto each pencil.

Colored Pencils

The early twentieth century saw the development of colored pencils, which are produced in much the same way as regular black-writing pencils. The difference is that the cores in colored pencils contain dyes and pigments instead of graphite. During the manufacturing of colored pencils, clay and gum are added to pigment as bonding agents. The mixture is then soaked in wax to make the pencils smoother. When the pencils have been formed, the outsides are painted according to the color of the center mixture.

Today, pencils are available in more than 70 colors, with 7 different yellows and 12 different blues. However, the black-writing pencil—manufactured at a pace of 6 billion per year in 40 different countries—continues to outsell all of its competitors, including colored pencils and the ballpoint pen.

THE "LEAD" PENCIL

In the early 1880s, the search for a pencil that didn't require sharpening led to the invention of what has variously been termed the automatic, propelling, repeating, or simply lead pencil. These instruments have a metal or plastic case and use leads similar to those found in wood-cased pencils. The lead, lodged in a metal spiral inside the case, is held in place by a rod with a metal stud fastened to it. When the cap is twisted, the rod and stud move downward in the spiral, forcing the lead toward the point.

A box of pencils, sharpened and ready for use.

Quality Control

Because they travel along a conveyor belt during the manufacturing process, pencils are looked over thoroughly before they are distributed to the public. Workers are trained to discard pencils that appear irregular, and a select number are sharpened and tested when the process is complete. A common problem is that the glue of the sandwiches sometimes doesn't adhere, but this nuisance is usually caught when the sandwiches are being cut.

WHERE TO LEARN MORE

Fischler, George. *Fountain Pens and Pencils.* Schiffer Publishing, 1990.

Leibson, Beth. "A Low-Tech Wonder," *Reader's Digest.* July 1992, p. 92.

Lord, Lewis J. "The Little Artifact that Could," *U.S. News & World Report.* January 22, 1990, p. 63.

Petroski, Henry. *The Pencil: A History of Design and Circumstance.* Knopf, 1990.

Sprout, Alison. "Recycled Pencil," *Fortune.* June 15, 1992, p. 113.

Thomson, Ruth. *Making Pencils.* Franklin Watts, 1987.

Perfume

Since the beginning of recorded history, humans have attempted to mask or enhance their own odor by using perfume, which imitates nature's pleasant smells. Many natural and manmade materials have been used to make perfume to apply to the skin and clothing, to put in cleaners and cosmetics, or to scent the air. Because of differences in body chemistry, temperature, and body odors, no perfume will smell exactly the same on any two people.

Perfume comes from the Latin *per,* meaning "through," and *fumum,* meaning "smoke." Many ancient perfumes were made by extracting natural oils from plants through pressing and steaming. The oil was then burned to scent the air. While fragrant liquids used for the body are often considered perfume, true (natural) perfumes are defined as extracts or essences and contain a percentage of oil distilled in alcohol. Water is also used. Today, most perfume is used to scent bar soaps. Some products are even perfumed with industrial odorants to mask unpleasant smells or to appear "unscented."

Because of differences in body chemistry, temperature, and body odors, no perfume will smell exactly the same on any two people.

Early Perfume

Ancient Egyptians burned incense called kyphi—made of henna (a brownish-red dye), myrrh (a gum obtained from trees and shrubs), cinnamon, and juniper (a type of evergreen tree or shrub)—as religious offerings. They soaked aromatic wood, gum, and resins in water and oil and used the liquid as a fragrant body lotion. Early Egyptians also perfumed their dead and often assigned specific fragrances to deities (gods). Their word for perfume has been translated as "fragrance of the gods." It is said

Many products that people use everyday are perfumed, including powders, soaps, and lotions.

In seventeenth-century England, aromatics were contained in lockets and the hollow heads of canes, to be sniffed by the owner.

that the Moslem prophet Mohammad wrote, "Perfumes are foods that reawaken the spirit."

According to the Bible, Three Wise Men visited the baby Jesus carrying frankincense (a tree gum) and myrrh. Eventually Egyptian perfumery influenced the Greeks and the Romans. For hundreds of years after the fall of Rome (A.D. 284-500), perfume was primarily an Oriental art. It spread to Europe when thirteenth-century Crusaders brought back samples from Palestine to England, France, and Italy. Europeans discovered the healing properties of fragrance during the seventeenth century. Doctors treating plague victims covered their mouths and noses with leather pouches holding pungent cloves, cinnamon, and other spices which were thought to protect the physicians from disease.

France's King Louis XIV (1659-1743) used perfume so much that he was called the "perfume king." His court contained a floral pavilion filled with fragrances, and dried flowers were placed in bowls throughout the palace to freshen the air. Royal guests bathed in goat's milk and rose petals. Visitors were often doused with perfume, which also was sprayed on clothing, furniture, walls, and tableware. It was at this time that Grasse, a region of southern France where many flowering plant varieties grow, became a leading producer of perfumes.

Synthetic Perfume

It was not until the late 1800s, when synthetic (manmade) chemicals were used, that perfumes could be mass-marketed. The first synthetic perfume was nitrobenzene, made from nitric acid and benzene. This synthetic mixture gave off an almond smell and was often used to scent soaps. In 1868, British chemist William Perkin (1838-1907) synthesized coumarin from the South American tonka bean to create a fragrance that smelled like freshly cut hay. Ferdinand Tiemann of the University of Berlin created synthetic violet and vanilla. In the United States, Francis Despard Dodge created citronellol—an alcohol with rose-like odor—by experimenting with citronella, which is derived from citronella oil and has a lemon-like odor. In different variations, this synthetic compound gives off the flower scents of sweet pea, lily of the valley, narcissus, and hyacinth.

Perfume Materials

Natural ingredients—flowers, grasses, spices, fruit, wood, roots, resins, balsams, leaves, gums, and animal secretions (such as musk)—as well as resources like alcohol, petrochemicals (chemicals derived from oil or natural gas), coal, and coal tars are used in the manufacture of perfumes. Some plants, such as lily of the valley, do not produce oils naturally. In fact, only about 2,000 of the 250,000 known flowering plant species contain these essential oils. Therefore, synthetic chemicals must be used to recreate the smells of non-oily substances. Synthetics also create original scents not found in nature.

Some perfume ingredients are animal products. For example, castor comes from beavers, musk from male deer, and ambergris from the sperm whale. Animal substances are often used as fixatives, which enable perfume to evaporate slowly and emit odors longer. Other fixatives include coal tar, mosses, resins, and synthetic chemicals. Alcohol and sometimes water are used to dilute ingredients in perfumes. It is the ratio of alcohol to scent that determines whether the result is *eau de toilette* (toilet water), perfume, or cologne. Contrary to popular belief, eau de toilette contains more essence and alcohol and less water than does cologne. Not only does the amount of the contents differ, but so does the price—a bottle of per-

Only about 2,000 of the 250,000 known flowering plant species contain the essential oils to make perfume.

fume runs from \$135 to \$350 an ounce, while a 1.7 ounce bottle of eau de toilette costs from \$19 to \$30, and the same size bottle of cologne costs from \$2 to \$21.

The Manufacturing Process

Before the manufacturing process begins, the initial ingredients must be collected and brought to the manufacturing center.

Collection

1 Plant substances are harvested from around the world, often hand-picked for their fragrance. Animal products are obtained by extracting the fatty substances directly from the animal. Aromatic chemicals used in synthetic perfumes are created in the laboratory by perfume chemists.

Extraction

2 Oils are extracted from plant substances by several methods: steam distillation, solvent extraction, enfleurage, maceration, and expression.

In steam distillation, steam is passed through plant material held in a still, whereby the essential oil turns to gas (see fig. 52). This gas is then passed through tubes, cooled, and liquefied. Oils can also be extracted by boiling plant substances like flower petals in water instead of steaming them.

Under solvent extraction, flowers are put into large rotating tanks or drums and benzene or a petroleum ether is poured over the flowers, extracting the essential oils (see fig. 52). The flower parts dissolve in the solvents and leave a waxy material that contains the oil, which is then placed in ethyl alcohol. The oil dissolves in the alcohol and rises. Heat is used to evaporate the alcohol, which once fully burned off, leaves a higher concentration of the perfume oil on the bottom.

During enfleurage, flowers are spread on glass sheets coated with grease (see fig. 53). The glass sheets are placed between wooden frames in tiers (layers). Then the flowers are removed by hand and changed until the grease has absorbed their fragrance.

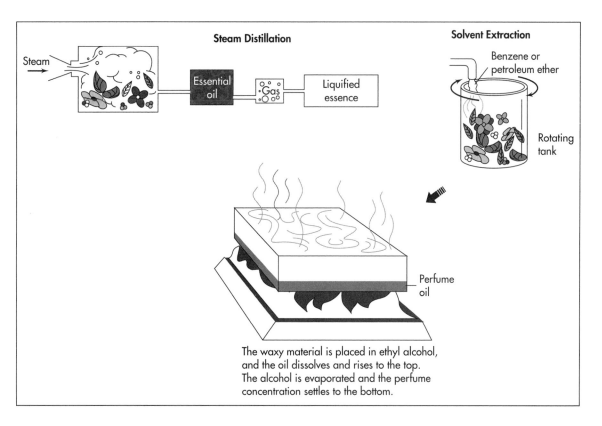

Fig. 52. During steam distillation, steam passing through plant materials change essential oils to gas and extract. In solvent extraction, flower parts dissolve in the solvents leaving a waxy material containing the oils.

Maceration is similar to enfleurage except that warmed fats are used to soak up the flower smell. As in solvent extraction, the grease and fats are dissolved in alcohol to obtain the essential oils.

Expression is the oldest and least complex method of extraction (see fig. 53). By this process, now used in obtaining citrus oils from the rind, the fruit or plant is manually or mechanically pressed until all the oil is squeezed out.

Thousands of flowers are needed to obtain just one pound of essential oils.

Blending

3 Once the perfume oils are collected, they are ready to be blended according to a formula determined by a master in the field, known as a "nose." It may take as many as 800 different ingredients and several years to develop the special formula for a scent.

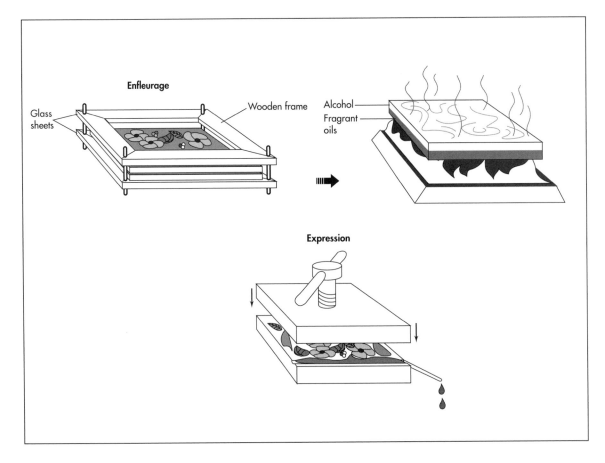

Fig. 53. The enfleurage process entails spreading flowers on glass sheets coated with grease and placed in wooden frames. Eventually the grease is dissolved in alcohol, which is then evaporated with heat to leave behind the oils. In the expression process, plant materials are pressed to squeeze out oils.

Perfume oils are blended together according to a formula determined by a master in the field, known as a "nose."

After the scent has been created, it is mixed with alcohol and water. The amount of scent can vary greatly. Most full perfumes are made up of about 15 to 30 percent perfume oils dissolved in alcohol and a trace of water. Typically, eau de toilette has 5-8 percent oil, while colognes contain approximately 2 to 7 percent oil diluted in larger portions of alcohol and water.

Aging

4 Fine perfume is often aged for several months or even years after it is blended. Following this, a "nose" will once again test the perfume to ensure that the correct scent has been achieved.

Perfume bottles come in many shapes and sizes. They are usually designed to give consumers a hint as to what type of scent is inside.

Packaging

5 Perfume packaging is as important, and sometimes more so, than the perfume itself. Most manufacturers hire designers to create bottles that reflect the fragrance inside, whether light and flowery or dark and musky. Depending on the design, some bottles are worth more empty a few years later than they were new.

Just as the art of perfumery progressed through the centuries, so did the art of the perfume bottle. Perfume bottles were often as elaborate and exotic as the oils they contained. The earliest specimens date back to about 1000 B.C. In ancient Egypt, newly invented glass bottles were made largely to hold perfumes. The crafting of perfume bottles spread into Europe and reached its peak in Venice, Italy, in the eighteenth century, when glass containers were made in the shape of small animals or had pastoral scenes painted on them.

It may take as many as 800 different ingredients and several years to develop the special formula for a scent.

*Each essential oil and perfume has three
notes: Notes de tete, or top notes; notes de
coeur, or central or heart notes; and notes
de fond, or base notes. Top notes have
tangy or citrus-like smells, central notes
(aromatic flowers like rose and jasmine) provide body, and base notes (woody fragrances) provide an enduring fragrance.*

*Naming a
perfume is so
competitive that
perfumers
copyright
thousands of
names to
prevent their
competitors from
using them.*

Naming the perfume is another important
element of packaging. It is a very secretive
process. Sometimes the nose, who is creating
the perfume, doesn't even know the name. Typically, the perfumer will select a name that is
easily pronounceable and memorable. Like the
bottle, the name usually reflects the scent and
the era.

Quality Control

Because perfumes depend heavily on harvests
of plant substances and the availability of animal products, making perfume can often turn
risky. Thousands of flowers are needed to obtain just one pound of essential oils, and if the season's crop is destroyed by disease or bad weather,
perfumeries can be in jeopardy. In addition, consistency is hard to maintain in natural oils. The same species of plant raised in several different
areas with slightly different growing conditions may not yield oils with
exactly the same scent.

Problems are also encountered in collecting natural animal oils. Many
animals once killed for the value of their oils are on the endangered
species list and now cannot be hunted. For example, sperm whale products like ambergris (a waxy material formed in the intestines) have been
banned by the United States. Also, most animal oils in general are difficult and expensive to extract. Some animals are raised in captivity specifically for their secretions: deer for deer musk in Tibet and China; civet
cats, bred in Ethiopia, are kept for their fatty gland secretions; and beavers
from Canada and the former Soviet Union are harvested for their castor
(a brown substance obtained from glands in beaver skin).

Synthetic scents have allowed perfumers more freedom and stability
in their craft, even though natural ingredients are considered more desir-
able in the very finest perfumes. The use of synthetic perfumes and oils
eliminates the need to extract oils from animals and removes the risk of a
poor plant harvest.

Future Perfume

Perfumes today are made and used in different ways than in previous
centuries. They are manufactured more frequently with synthetic

chemicals, and less concentrated forms of perfume are becoming increasingly popular. Combined, these factors decrease the cost of the scents, encouraging more widespread and frequent (often daily) use.

Using perfume to heal and to make people feel good are new frontiers being re-explored by the industry. Aromatherapy—smelling oils and fragrances to cure physical and emotional problems—is being revived to help balance hormonal and body energy. The theory behind aromatherapy is that using essential oils helps bolster the immune system when the oils are inhaled or applied topically. Sweet smells also affect one's mood and can be used as a form of psychotherapy.

Differences between men's and women's perfumes are also changing. Usually perfume is made for and marketed to one gender or the other. A new trend by some perfume makers is to market unisex scents, or the same fragrance that can be worn by either gender. Similarly, some perfumers market to males and females separately, but create almost the same scent. For those who still prefer to wear traditional feminine or masculine scents, there are almost 800 kinds on the shelves from which to choose.

WHERE TO LEARN MORE

Green, Timothy. "Making Scents Is More Complicated Than You Think," *Smithsonian.* June 1991, pp. 52-60.

"How to Buy a Fragrance," *Consumer Reports.* December 1993, pp. 765-73.

Iverson, Annemarie. "Ozone," *Harper's Bazaar.* November 1993, pp. 208-40.

Lord, Shirley. "Message In a Bottle," *Vogue.* May 1992, p. 220.

Meier, Raymon. "Fragrance Force," *Harper's Bazaar.* April 1995, pp. 209-11, 234.

Raphael, Anna. "Ahh! Aromatherapy," *Delicious!* December 1994, pp. 47-48.

Starzinger, Page Hill. "The Story of Eaux," *Harper's Bazaar.* March 1995, pp 92, 96.

Photographic Film

Photographic film is a chemically reactive material that records an image when the film is exposed to light. For many years after the invention of the camera, photography was limited to professionals because film and camera equipment were difficult to use. With the invention of roll film in the late nineteenth century, and advanced camera technology, taking a picture has become as easy as pressing a button. Today, more than 90 percent of U.S. households own cameras, accounting for more than 847 million rolls of film purchased per year.

More than 90 percent of all U.S. households own cameras, and buy more than 847 million rolls of film per year.

Early Film

Film was "discovered" in a chemistry laboratory. In 1727, Johann Heinrich Schulze, a German doctor, mixed chalk, silver, and nitric acid in a flask to make silver nitrate. When the solution was exposed to sunlight, it changed color from white to purple. When Schulze pasted cutouts of letters and numbers on the outside of a flask of freshly made solution and exposed it to the light, the cutouts appeared to have been printed on the solution. Although the discovery marked the birth of photography, it was not used for over 100 years.

In 1839, Louis Daguerre, a French painter, created a photographic process in which liquid iodine was placed on a silvered copper plate, and

Eastman's gelatine (gelatin) dry plates, a photographic process used in the late 1800s.

the plate was exposed to light. The liquid iodine was the emulsion, or light-reactive chemical, and the copper plate was the base for these photographs called "daguerreotypes." Daguerreotypy, however, was cumbersome to use; the "wet plate" process was awkward, the box-type cameras had to hold the large plates, and the finished photographs came in only one size—the size of the plates.

While Daguerre was developing his process, William Henry Fox Talbot, an English archaeologist, created his own process in 1841 called *calotype,* meaning "beautiful picture." Talbot coated a paper base with an emulsion of silver iodide and produced a negative by a developing process. The calotype is more like today's film and photographic process, and the intermediate step resulting in a negative permitted more than one print to be made.

The flexibility of photography was improved further in 1871 when Richard Leach Maddox invented the "dry plate" process. Gelatin made from animal bones and hides was used to coat glass plates, and silver

The first Kodak camera, introduced in 1888. This particular camera was owned by Miss Celine McKee of Indianapolis, Indiana.

iodide was put inside the gelatin layer. The plates and their dried jelly could be exposed (by taking a picture); the photograph could be developed later, instead of right away like previous methods, by rewetting the gelatin. The complicated procedure of manufacturing the plate, exposing it, and processing it into the finished photograph was broken into parts that made the photographer's work easier and made photography and photo processing a manufacturing industry.

Later Developments

Although photography improved over the years, it was still a relatively difficult and expensive process. Photographers had to carry and set up a large and heavy camera (about 20 to 30 pounds), work with noxious chemicals, and handle heavy glass plates that were easily broken. Moreover, developing the photographs was still the photographer's responsibility. Because of these reasons, photography attracted few beginners— that is, until inventor George Eastman (1854-1932) got into the picture.

In search of better photographic tools, Eastman combined the paper base of Talbot's calotype with the gelatinous silver nitrate emulsion from Maddox's process to invent flexible roll film in 1884. He quickly made the transition to a cellulose, transparent film by 1889, which was a year after his company introduced the first Kodak camera. Eastman's motto, "You press the button, we do the rest," meant that owners no longer had to worry about loading or developing the film themselves—the 100-frame film was already loaded inside the camera. Once the film was used up, the photographer shipped the entire camera to the Eastman Dry Plate and Film Company in Rochester, New York, for developing. The company would then send back the developed prints and the camera reloaded with another 100 shots.

Although Eastman's process was convenient, it was too expensive for most people at the time. The camera and film cost about $25 and another $10 was required for developing. Realizing this, Eastman continued to make smaller, less expensive cameras. By 1900 he introduced the Brownie—a small, portable, easy-to-operate camera that cost only $1. Additional rolls of six-exposure film cost only $.15 each. Even though it was up to the photographer to install, rewind, and remove the film for developing, it was easy to do. Eastman's improved camera and film made photography a simple, portable practice, one that has grown to be one of the most popular hobbies in the United States.

How Photo Film Works

Typically, film is placed inside a camera and advanced to the first exposure. To take a picture, a person just aims and shoots (that is, of course, when using a compact—automatic everything—camera). Pressing the button opens the camera's shutter (a device that opens and shuts the lens opening), which exposes the film to the image and to light. A combination of how fast the shutter opens and closes and the film speed (determined by how much light is needed to capture the image) controls the amount of light that strikes the film. Although the image is recorded on the film, it does not become visible until the film is removed from the camera and developed by chemical processes.

GEORGE EASTMAN HOUSE

Although Eastman Kodak no longer gives public plant tours, the George Eastman House offers a wealth of information about Eastman, who lived in the mansion from 1905-1932, and his company. In addition to the mansion tour there is the International Museum of Photography and Film (attached to the mansion), which houses a large collection of photography, film, technology, and literature. For more information on either tour, call or write to:

George Eastman House
900 East Avenue
Rochester, NY 14607
(716) 271-3361

Choosing the right 35-mm film—the most common film used—can be difficult since there are over 120 types on the market.

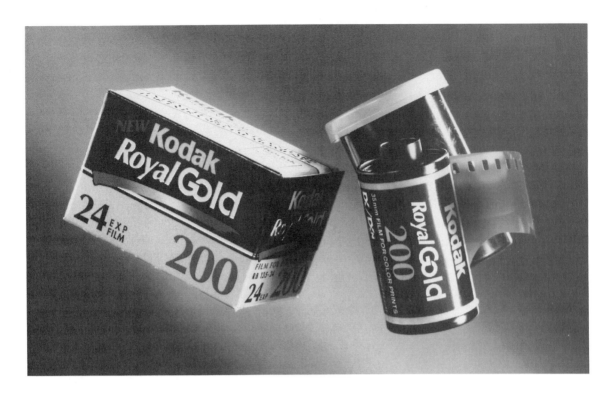

Kodak's Royal Gold 35-millimeter film with a speed of 200 is an example of the most common film used by amateur photographers.

After the image appears, the film is called a negative. A negative is an image in which light areas appear dark and the dark areas appear light. The image is made positive, or as our eyes see it, by another type of processing that prints the negative on sensitive paper. Color-reversal films are positives and are used for making slides. All of the elements of the process—the parts of the camera, the type and parts of the lens, the type of film and its chemistry, the developing process, the printing process, and the type of paper—contribute to the sharpness or trueness of the finished photograph.

Film comes in a variety of speeds, starting with an ISO number (set by the International Standards Organization) as slow as 25 and up to a really fast speed of 3,200. The ISO rating of a film indicates its sensitivity to light and image quality. For example, ISO 25 to 50 is ultra slow, which means it is not very sensitive to light and needs to be exposed to light longer. It also means that the image quality will be good—almost grainless (free of unwanted markings, patterns, or textures) and razor sharp.

This film speed is ideal when there is a lot of surrounding light. Fast film with an ISO 200 to 400 rating can be used in a wide variety of lighting situations, although coarser grain and weaker colors become noticeable. Ultrafast film with speeds over 1,000 is ideal for taking pictures in low light. The pictures, however, appear very grainy. Choosing a speed of film depends on the lighting available and the image effect desired.

Keeping photographic film in the refrigerator or freezer will slow the deterioration of the film in regard to color accuracy, saturation, and structure. Refrigeration—the colder the better—sometimes allows the film to be used after its expiration date. Film should never be inserted into the camera while it's still cold; it should be room temperature. Film needs 1 hour to warm up from refrigeration—1½ hours if it was in the freezer—before it is loaded into the camera.

Film Materials

A roll of film consists of the emulsion and base that compose the film itself, the cassette or cartridge, and outer protective packaging. The materials used to make the emulsion are silver, nitric acid, and gelatin. The base consists of cellulose and solvents that are mixed to form a thick fluid called dope. Film that is packed in a cassette (35-millimeter film is typically packed this way) requires a metal spool, the protective metal canister, and plastic strips at the canister opening where the film emerges. Other sizes of film, including Polaroid film (film that develops itself within a few minutes after the picture is taken) used with a Polaroid camera (invented in 1948), are protected from light and air by plastic cartridges or packs. Outer packaging, which varies among film products, is made from foil-lined paper, plastic, and thin cardboard cartons. The outer packaging is also insulating and protects the film from exposure to light, heat, and air.

The Manufacturing Process

Base

1 For most films, the base to which the light-sensitive emulsion is fixed consists of cellulose acetate, which is wood pulp or cotton linters (short cottonseed fibers) mixed with acetate (a salt) to form a syrup (see fig. 54). Solid pellets of cellulose acetate precipitate out of the syrup and are washed and dried. The pellets are dissolved in solvents to form the transparent, honey-like dope. The dope is spread in a thin, even sheet on a large rotating wheel (see fig. 54). The wheel is plated with chromium for a smooth finish, and it turns slowly. The solvents in the dope

American inventor Samuel F. B. Morse learned the art of daguerreotypy and taught it to photographer Matthew Brady, who made images of the Civil War (1861-65) that are treasured as historical records and as artistic landmarks in photography.

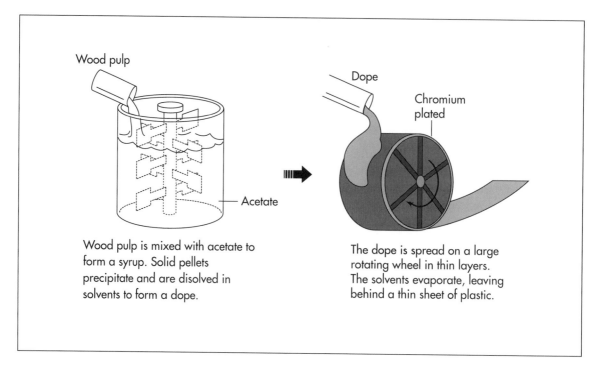

Wood pulp

Dope

Chromium plated

Acetate

Wood pulp is mixed with acetate to form a syrup. Solid pellets precipitate and are disolved in solvents to form a dope.

The dope is spread on a large rotating wheel in thin layers. The solvents evaporate, leaving behind a thin sheet of plastic.

Fig. 54. Making the base.

volatilize, or evaporate, as the wheel turns. The process is much like the applying and drying of **nail polish** (see entry in Series I). The remaining base is a thin sheet of plastic with a uniform thickness measured in ten-thousandths of an inch. When it is dry, the base is removed from the wheel and wound on 54-inch (137-centimeter) diameter reels.

Emulsion

2 Silver is the main ingredient of the emulsion. Pure silver bullion is received at the manufacturing plant in bars that are checked by weight and serial number. The bars are dissolved in a strong solution of nitric acid, and the process releases heat (see fig. 55). After the acid has completely dissolved the silver, the solution is stirred constantly and cooled. Cooling causes crystals of silver nitrate to grow, much like salt crystals in water. The crystals are wet with water that also separates out. The crystals are removed from the solution and whirled in centrifuges (a machine that separates substances by rotating them at high speeds) with sieve-like openings to remove the water and keep the crystals pure. At

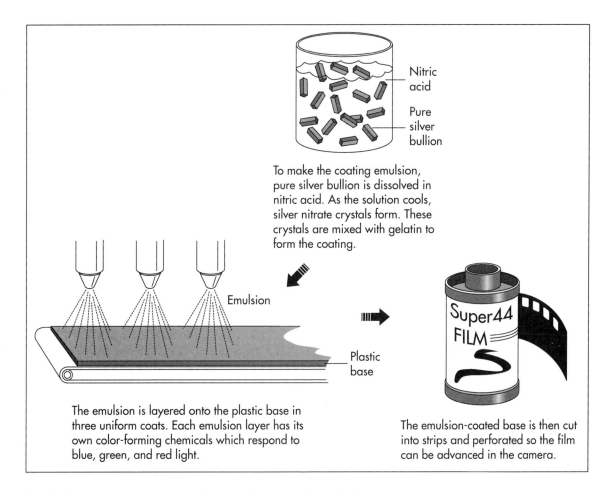

To make the coating emulsion, pure silver bullion is dissolved in nitric acid. As the solution cools, silver nitrate crystals form. These crystals are mixed with gelatin to form the coating.

The emulsion is layered onto the plastic base in three uniform coats. Each emulsion layer has its own color-forming chemicals which respond to blue, green, and red light.

The emulsion-coated base is then cut into strips and perforated so the film can be advanced in the camera.

Fig. 55. The coating emulsion, and the emulsion-coated base (film).

this point in the process, the chemical solutions are light-sensitive, so further manufacturing processes are completed in darkness.

3 Meanwhile, gelatin has been made using distilled water and treated with chemicals including potassium iodide and potassium bromide. The gelatin serves as a binding agent to hold the silver nitrate crystals, and also to fix them to the base. The gelatin and chemicals are mixed in cookers that are lined with silver so the emulsion remains pure. As the mixture cools, silver halide salts (chemical combinations of the silver,

iodide, and bromide) form as fine crystals that remain suspended in the gelatin to make the emulsion.

Coating process

4 The emulsion is pumped through a piping system to "coating alley," a huge work area that may be 200 feet (61 meters) wide and five stories high. The area must be immaculately clean and dust-free, and the operations of the roll-coating machines are controlled by arrays of control panels in the fully automated process. Machines coat precise amounts of emulsion in micro-thin layers on the wide strips of plastic base; a single, dried layer of emulsion may be six one-hundred-thousandths of an inch thick (see fig. 55). Successive layers of three emulsions are applied to the base to make color film, and each emulsion layer has its own color-forming chemicals called linked dyes. The three emulsion layers in color film respond to blue, green, and red light, so each photograph is a triple hidden image with the sandwiched color range reproduced by processing.

5 The strips of emulsion-coated base (now film) are cut into progressively narrower widths, perforated so the film can be advanced in the camera, and spooled, except for instant film and sheet film that are packed flat (see fig. 55).

Packaging

5 Film is packed in cartridges, cassettes, rolls, instant packs, or sheets. Cartridges (mostly used with 110 and 126 film—like 35-millimeter, these numbers refer to image size) include a take-up spool that is built in so the exposed film and cartridge can be removed as one unit. Cassettes are for cameras that use film in the 35-millimeter format. They consist of a spool enclosed in a metal jacket with a piece of the film, called a leader, sticking out. The leader is inserted into a built-in take-up spool, which helps to advance the film. When the film is finished, it is rewound onto the cassette spool and removed.

Roll films are paper-backed film that is packed on a spool like the one in the camera. The film is wound onto the spool in the camera, and that spool and film are removed. The spool on which the film was packed originally can then be moved to the receiving side of the camera, and a new roll inserted. The packs for instant cameras by Polaroid contain 8 to 12 sheets of film that are ejected individually after each shot. Sheet film is used for specialized applications like X-ray film.

After being packaged in its proper container, the film is wrapped in additional packaging such as foil-lined paper pouches and then the outer cartons. The packaging is dated, shrink-wrapped in plastic in quantities appropriate for sale, packed in cardboard containers for shipping, and stored in air-conditioned rooms to await shipment.

Quality Control

In all phases of manufacture, photographic film is extremely sensitive to light, heat, dust, and impurities. Air that flows into the film-manufacturing rooms is washed and filtered. Temperature and humidity are carefully regulated. Production rooms are scrubbed clean daily, and plant workers wear protective clothing and enter sensitive work areas through air showers that remove dust and contaminants. Each step of manufacture is carefully inspected and controlled. For example, the chromium-plated wheel on which the base is formed is inspected to maintain a mirror-like finish because tiny imperfections will affect the quality of the film. Finally, samples of film are removed from completed batches and subjected to many tests, including the taking of photographs.

Most plastic film containers carry the "Number 2" recycling symbol, and can therefore be recycled with milk jugs and other plastic containers. The film containers are also good for crafts or for storing small items such as pins or coins.

Byproducts/Waste

Factory workers and the environment must be protected from the hazardous chemicals, fumes, and wastes that can be generated while making film. Protective clothing keeps the product clean and insulates the workers from possible contaminants. Air released to the outside is also filtered and monitored. Extensive recycling is done, not only to protect the environment but also to salvage valuable materials such as silver for purifying and reuse. The photographic film industry was among the first to use incineration successfully to burn wastes efficiently and control emissions.

Future Film

Manufacturers are continually improving the quality of film so that photographs are sharper, color is truer, graininess is reduced, and film speed is improved. Several new camera films use "T-grain" emulsion technology, in which the molecular structure of the silver halide crystals is modified to create silver grains shaped like tiny tablets. The flat shape helps them collect light efficiently, so sharper photographs are produced from higher-speed films. This technology also benefits the environment because fewer chemicals are needed for processing film, and the opportunity for chemicals to enter the environment is reduced.

Chemists at the University of Osaka in Japan are working on reusable photographic film, in which the image on the exposed frame could be dissolved and another exposure made on the same frame. More work is needed, however, to determine how long images made by the process will last.

Film and camera manufacturers have just come out with a new film and camera technology called the Advanced Photo System. The 35-millimeter leaderless film is easy to load and ensures that the photographer does not thread the film incorrectly. Along with the film are new cameras (the new film does not fit current camera models) and new developing methods. New camera features allow the photographer to specify different print sizes electronically and to label photos with the date and time the photo was taken or even a short caption. A new developing process eliminates negatives. Instead, people receive a full color index, or a postcard-size sheet of small, numbered versions of each shot on a roll, which makes it easier for the consumer to pick prints for enlargement or duplication.

The next advance in photography also requires a new type of camera, but one that needs no film. The film-free camera stores photographs digitally and electronically transfers images to computers which can then print the images. Digital photography may not replace traditional photography, but it will certainly give it a new perspective.

WHERE TO LEARN MORE

Antonoff, Michael. "Digital Snapshots from My Vacation," *Popular Science.* June 1995, pp. 72-76.

Bailey, Adrian and Adrian Holloway. *The Book of Color Photography.* Alfred A. Knopf, 1979.

Collins, Douglas. *The Story of Kodak.* Harry N. Abrams, Inc., Publishers, 1990.

Frost, Lee. *Teach Yourself Photography.* NTC Publishing Group, 1993.

Holusha, John. "Photo Industry Strikes Back: New Cameras and Film to Counter the Camcorder," *New York Times.* November 25, 1995, pp. Y17, Y21.

Player Piano

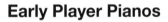

The modern player piano begins as a standard acoustic piano with a keyboard. When the keys are struck, felt hammers strike tuned metal strings to create musical tones. The intricate collection of felt hammers and connecting parts is called the "piano action." The piano action can be manipulated either with the musician's fingers or by a player system installed on the piano.

Early Player Pianos

Early player pianos were known to have been built by piano builder Samuel Bidermann (1540-1622) of Augsburg, Germany. During his lifetime, he equipped three spinets (small, upright pianos) with pinned barrels similar to those in music boxes.

Interest in inventing a self-playing piano did not resurface until the late 1890s. Several different mechanisms were developed and sold using paper rolls, but the rolls were not interchangeable. Melville Clark (1850-1918), an inventor and piano designer from New York, developed an 88-note, standardized roll size for the player industry, and built his Apollo player piano to this standard in 1901. By 1908, other manufacturers had adopted his standard. Duplicating machines called perforators punched the paper rolls from a master roll used as a pattern. The master rolls were tediously hand-punched by skilled workers directly from sheet music. To avoid this production difficulty, Clark invented the "marking piano" in 1912.

Clarke's marking piano punched the master roll data as the musician performed a piece of music. The marking piano was used from 1912-31. Historic performances by artists of the day were preserved in live record-

The player piano must be able to play a wide range of music, so a large music library in software form has also been developed and updated.

In 1958, Ed Landrum of Dallas, Texas, built his own "modernized" player piano, replacing the foot-pumping system with electronics.

ings, and the marking piano made the Roaring Twenties the heyday of the player piano until the popularity of the phonograph and radio surpassed it. In 1926, the player piano's peak sales year, more than 10 million piano rolls were sold. The marking piano was retired in 1931, restored in 1971 to record the performances of other outstanding artists, and designated a National Historic Mechanical Engineering Landmark in 1992. Following all-time low sales in the 1950s, roll-player pianos experienced a revival in the 1970s, and traditional player pianos and paper rolls are still manufactured and sold.

PLAYER-PIANO ROLLS

QRS Music Rolls is the world's oldest and largest mass manufacturer of player-piano rolls. For information on seeing player-piano rolls made, call or write to:

QRS Music Rolls
1026 Niagara Street
Buffalo, NY 14213-2099
(716) 885-4600

How Roll-Player Pianos Work

The traditional, roll-operated player piano has a pneumatic (air-driven) player action that operates the piano. Attached to each piano key is a striker that resembles a miniature bellows (a device for pumping air that inflates and deflates like an accordion). As each striker is pneumatically collapsed, its corresponding key is pushed to play. The full set of strikers makes up the player action. The player action "reads music" by detecting coded perforations, or holes, in paper rolls. This detection is done by a system of tubes and valves and, as the perforations are noted, the pneumatic system tells the strikers when to collapse. An electric vacuum motor or pedals that are pumped by foot supply the air, or pneumatic power.

The roll-player piano has several disadvantages. The player action must be built into the piano during assembly; it cannot be added later. Also, the pneumatic strikers push their keys at one dynamic (force) level only, so the notes of the music are heard, but without soft or loud variations.

Components such as digital cassette drives and computers enable the acoustic piano to be played using electronic "brains" and power.

Today's Player Piano

In the 1920s, experiments began with electric or electromagnetic devices instead of the piano soundboard. Electronic pianos, keyboards, and music synthesizers use electronic circuits or tuned metal pieces instead of strings to produce sound. Some generate sounds approaching those of a conventional piano, but they are most valued for producing effects that are electronically altered from the acoustic piano voice. Electronic applications began to merge with the acoustic piano in the 1970s. The acoustic piano (as opposed to the electronic piano) was equipped with components such as digital cassette drives or computers to enable it to be played using electronic "brains" and power.

Several major manufacturers now produce disc-driven player pianos, and systems and software are sold in kits to convert acoustic pianos to players. The instrument that has been idle since grade-school piano lessons can thus be converted to an entertainment center. The remainder of this article will focus on the manufacture of the disc-driven piano.

How Modern Player Pianos Work

The modern player piano has a player action that uses electronically driven solenoids as strikers. A solenoid is a tubular coil that acts like a magnet when an electric current passes through it. Solenoids respond to signals from a Musical Instrument Digital Interface or MIDI, which is the universal electronic language spoken by keyboards, music synthesizers, and other electronic instruments. The MIDI plays both the notes and dynamics as recorded by the musician. Libraries of recorded music are stored on **floppy disk**s (see entry in Series I) or **compact disc**s (see entry in Series I) so the piano can play virtually any piece of music. If equipped with appropriate software and electronics, the player piano can also play recorded vocalists, instruments, or a full symphony orchestra. Thanks to the common MIDI language, it can be linked to sequencers, drum machines, and synthesizers as well as computers.

Design

Engineers design the player piano system and develop new products. A new system or application begins with a concept that is developed and designed. The manufacturer's legal staff, meanwhile, performs a thorough patent search so that new approaches do not infringe on existing patents, and the firm's own original concepts can be patented promptly. Prototypes are hand-assembled, tested, and evaluated for marketability and feasibility of construction. The engineers provide design details and specifications for every component of the product, including electrical, electronic, and mechanical parts; tooling and special machining or assem-

A disc-driven player piano. The small black box at the right under the keys looks something like the CD player one uses to play to music at home. Although this one uses only floppy disks, disc-driven player pianos can also use compact discs. Photo courtesy of Hammell Music, Redford, Michigan.

bly; and requirements for operation, installation, testing, maintenance, and repair. Because few parts may be made on site, the search for parts or suppliers capable of manufacturing them may be worldwide.

Software engineers must also provide the programming so that computer chips can convert notes and data representing musical expressions into electronic signals that drive the solenoids. More than 1,000 pages of computer code may be required for this complicated communication.

To appeal to a broad market, the player piano must be able to play a wide range of music, so a large music library in software form has also been developed and updated. The "codes" from traditional player piano rolls don't translate easily to the MIDI language, but actual performances are ideally suited to the digital system because they convey interpretive elements. Manufacturers maintain their own recording studios and recruit name performers to play their piano styles. Music editors review the recorded performances, correct any errors or inconsistencies, or modify performances in accordance with musical scores, as appropriate. The legal staff secures contracts, releases, and licenses to the music and performances.

Player Piano Materials

Essentially no raw materials are used in the manufacture of disc-driven player pianos. Manufacturers provide specifications to vendors and then purchase required parts from them. These parts may include factory-produced acoustic pianos in which the player systems are installed.

The Manufacturing Process

Player subassembly

The player subassembly is the player action that consists of 88 solenoids and plungers, computer-activated to move the keys. It is made of pre-existing parts that are put together along an assembly line using a combination of hand-assembly and automated processes.

1 The electronics, including the power supply, control box, key activation devices, and interconnections, are controlled by the components on a printed circuit board. Circuit boards in panel form (multiple boards of the same kind made on one large panel and separated after components are inserted) are used to facilitate automated assembly because components can be added easily. Components of a single kind are supplied in long rolls that are fed through an automated sequencer. The sequencer checks to make sure each part is correct, then organizes an

Leveling the keys on a player piano.

array of parts into the proper sequence for insertion in the circuit board. Some parts are formed, shaped, and inserted in the board by an automated dip inserter that can also check the appropriateness of the part. Other parts are added by hand.

2 The parts are soldered (joined using melted metal) in place by passing the circuit board through a wave soldering machine. It washes the board with flux (a substance used to remove contaminants), heats the board and components by infrared heat to reduce thermal (heat) shock as the board is soldered, then passes the underside of the board over a wave of molten solder. Afterwards, the solder cools and hardens, fixing the components in place.

3 The completed circuit boards are installed in control boxes and tested as a quality assurance step. Software is loaded and the control boxes are activated over a two-day test period, or "burn-in" process, that simulates the actual working of the player system. Any failures during that time are detected and corrected.

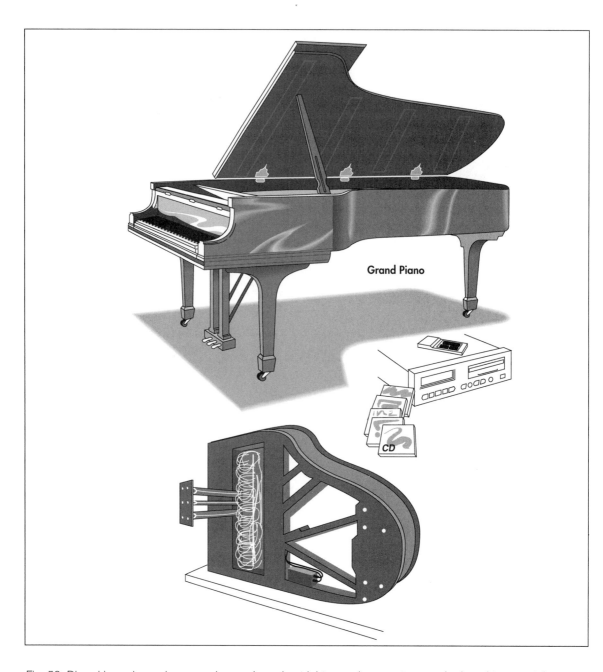

Fig. 56. Disc-driven player pianos can be purchased outright or a player system can be bought separately as a kit and installed on a regular piano.

4 On another part of the player subassembly line, the solenoids and plungers are made and installed on a rail or support. Magnetic wire is wrapped by machine on the solenoid bases and sealed in place. Wire connections are also attached to each solenoid, and the plunger assemblies are paired with solenoids. The solenoids and plungers are assembled on aluminum rails. Depending on the manufacturer, the solenoid/plungers vary in configuration, and the rail may be one piece or several sections. Rail mounting brackets will be used later to mount the solenoids under the piano keyboard. A similar assembly is made to activate the piano pedals.

Disc-driven systems are available in kits, which can be used to retrofit standard pianos to players.

Recording strip

The player piano can also record music played on the piano if a recording strip is installed; this allows students or performers to play back their work and aids composers in creating and revising their compositions.

5 The recording strip consists of a mounting rail and tiny electronic film switches that are cased in plastic. There is one switch or finger per key; the recording strip is sensitive to the key or keys that are struck, the duration they are depressed, and the velocity or intensity (soft or loud) per key strike. The recording strip is linked electronically to the piano's computer, where signals are processed into MIDI messages. This data can be stored by analog media like a cassette player or VCR, or directed to a floppy disk drive. It can be played back by the piano or other MIDI-compatible instrument.

Disc-player

6 The disc-player and other devices are connected to the player piano via the control box (see fig. 56). It may be a floppy disk drive, compact disc (CD) player, or both; player pianos can also be attached to VCRs in combination with televisions or computer monitors so lyrics can be synchronized for sing-alongs or other programmed entertainment. Most manufacturers purchase these components and remote controls for them from outside suppliers.

Accompaniment and speakers

7 As an added feature, the player piano can play along with all manner of recorded accompaniments including vocals, individual instruments, or an orchestra. The "soundboxes" for these additions are electronic speakers that can be furnished as accessories to the piano and

Player pianos can also be attached to VCRs in combination with televisions or computer monitors so lyrics can be synchronized for sing-alongs or other programmed entertainment.

that are supplied by vendors. Software is added to supply the other sounds via the MIDI system.

Piano installation

8 On another assembly line, the player subassembly and recording strip are installed in a piano. The pianos are supplied by the manufacturer's own piano division or an outside vendor. A slot is cut in the wood under the piano keyboard, but the structural integrity of the piano is not affected. The solenoid rail or set of rails is mounted under the piano so that the plungers are under the tails of the keys. The recording strip is similarly installed. The solenoid links with the pedals are also connected, the control box is mounted under the keyboard, and the power supply is mounted to the underside of the piano. The piano action must be adjusted at this point. The keys rest on felt pads that compress with use, so the pianos are programmed to play overnight in another burn-in process. After a 12-hour "concert," the felt has compressed. Then the components are checked to see that they have worked properly, and the piano action is adjusted to suit the felt compression. The pianos are packed and shipped when installation is complete.

Kit assembly

9 Some manufacturers provide their disc-driven systems in kits that can be used to retrofit standard pianos to players. As the completed subassemblies, control boxes and power supplies, and recording strips come off the assembly lines, they are packaged and stored. Kits are then packed with these units as well as disc-players and accessories. The kits are shipped to installers who have been specially trained to install the particular manufacturer's system. Installation typically takes up to two days, including an overnight burn-in session after which the piano action is adjusted and component workings are checked as they are in the factory.

Quality Control

Quality control is essential in every production step. As parts are received from vendors around the world, they are checked for compliance with

Making the final adjustments to the roll on a new player piano.

specifications and other engineering requirements. Along the player sub-assembly line, workers perform quality checks as part of their responsibility. For example, as circuit boards emerge from the wave soldering machine, the operator inspects the board to see that parts have been soldered in place, no bridging of solder has occurred from one component to another, and the board itself has not warped or cracked. The operator also monitors the machine for temperature of the solder and overall operation of the machine. Electronic assemblies must also meet the requirements of Underwriters' Laboratories (UL). UL representatives visit the manufacturers frequently and randomly check for compliance with their materials, operations, and safety codes. Other quality checks, such as the burn-ins of control boxes and piano actions, are integrated into the manufacturing process, as previously described.

Future Player Pianos

Acoustic pianos are instruments long favored by listeners, and their future is assured by the disc-driven player piano which provides the sounds and entertainment benefits without requiring the listener to become a virtuoso, or master. Disc-driven player pianos have initiated substantial increases in the sales of pianos, and are seen as the growth sector of the industry. In the disc-driven player piano's future, manufacturers are striving to reproduce performance nuances. Continued merging of technologies also seems likely as professional recording studios are used to input music and as methods are found of linking the player piano to other electronic media.

WHERE TO LEARN MORE

Goldberg, Ron. "I Got Immortality," *Popular Science.* March 1994, p. 42.

Matzer, Marla. "Play It Again," *Forbes.* February 27, 1995, pp. 138-39.

Slutsker, G. "The Player Piano Makes a Comeback," *Forbes.* September 4, 1989, p. 124.

Thompson, Terri. "A Virtuoso Ghost at the Keyboard," *U.S. News & World Report.* January 14, 1991, pp. 60-61.

Rubber Band

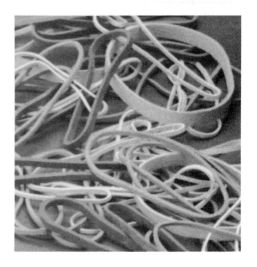

Rubber bands, sometimes called elastics, are for a wide variety of purposes. For example, the U.S. Post Office, which is the largest consumer of rubber bands in the world, orders millions of pounds a year for its mail sorting and delivery operations. The newspaper industry also buys massive quantities of rubber bands for fastening rolled or folded newspapers. To secure flowers, fruits, and vegetables the agricultural industry uses various types of rubber bands. All in all, more than 30 million pounds of rubber bands are sold in the United States alone each year.

More than 30 million pounds of rubber bands are sold in the United States each year.

History of Rubber

In the late 1400s, while exploring what are now the Americas, Christopher Columbus encountered Mayan Indians using waterproof shoes and bottles made from a rubbery substance. Intrigued, he carried several Mayan rubber items on his return voyage to Europe. Over the next several hundred years, other European explorers followed suit. The word "rubber" was born in 1770, when an English chemist named Joseph Priestley discovered that hardened pieces of rubber would rub out pencil marks. By the late eighteenth century, European scientists had discovered that dissolving rubber in turpentine produced a liquid that could be used to waterproof cloth.

Until the beginning of the nineteenth century, natural rubber presented several technical challenges. While it clearly had the potential for development, no one was able to get it to the point where it could be used commercially. Rubber rapidly became dry and brittle during cold European winters. Worse, it became soft and sticky when warm.

The largest consumer of rubber bands in the world is the U.S. Post Office, which orders millions of pounds a year to use in sorting and delivering piles of mail.

Birth of Vulcanization

American inventor Charles Goodyear had been experimenting with methods to refine natural rubber for nearly a decade before a fortunate accident occurred. One day in 1839, Goodyear accidentally left a piece of raw rubber on top of a warm stove, along with some sulfur and lead. On discovering his "mistake," Goodyear realized that the rubber now had a much more usable consistency and texture. Over the next five years, he perfected the process of converting natural rubber into a usable commodity. This process, which Goodyear dubbed vulcanization (after Vulcan, the Roman god of fire), made the modern rubber industry possible.

First Patents

The first rubber band was developed in 1843, when an Englishman named Thomas Hancock sliced up a rubber bottle made by some Native Americans. Although these first rubber bands were adapted as garters and waistbands, their usefulness was limited because they were unvulcanized. Hancock himself never vulcanized his invention, but he did advance the rubber industry by developing the masticator machine, a forerunner of the modern rubber milling machine used to manufacture rubber bands and other rubber products.

In 1845, another Englishman named Thomas Perry patented the rubber band and opened the first rubber-band factory. With the combined contributions of Goodyear, Hancock, and Perry, effective rubber bands could be manufactured.

In the late nineteenth century, British rubber manufacturers began to develop rubber plantations in British colonies, like Malaya and Ceylon. Rubber plantations thrived in the warm climate of Southeast Asia, and the European rubber industry thrived as well. More importantly, Britain could avoid the expense of importing rubber from the Americas, which lay beyond its political and economic control.

Rubber Band Materials

Although 75 percent of today's rubber products are made from the synthetic rubber perfected during World War II (1939-45), rubber bands are still made from natural rubber because it offers superior elasticity. Natural rubber comes from latex, a milky fluid composed primarily of water with a smaller amount of rubber and trace amounts of resin, protein, sugar, and mineral matter. Most natural industrial latex comes from the rubber tree, but other trees, shrubs, and vines also produce the substance.

The Manufacturing Process

Processing the natural latex

1 The initial stage of manufacturing the harvested latex usually takes place on the rubber plantation, prior to packing and shipping. The first step in processing the latex is purification, or straining it to remove impurities such as tree sap and debris.

2 The purified rubber is now collected in large vats. Combined with acetic or formic acid, the rubber particles cling together to form slabs.

3 Next, the slabs are squeezed between rollers to remove excess water (see fig. 57) and pressed into bales or blocks, usually 2 or 3 feet square (.6 or .9 meters square), ready for shipping to factories.

Mixing and milling

4 Once at the rubber factory, the slabs are machine cut (or chopped) into small pieces. Next, many manufacturers use a Banbury mixer, to mix the rubber with other ingredients—sulfur to vulcanize it, pigments to color it, and other chemicals to increase or diminish the elasticity of the resulting rubber bands (see fig. 57). Although some companies don't add these ingredients until the next stage (milling), the Banbury machine mixes them better, producing a more uniform product.

5 Milling, the next phase of production, involves heating the rubber (a blended mass if it has been mixed, separate pieces if it has not) and flattening it in a milling machine.

EXTRACTING RUBBER

Latex is found in veins between the outside bark and the Cambium layer (where the sap flows) inside the rubber tree. Distinct from the sap, latex serves as a protective agent, seeping out of and sealing over wounds in the tree's bark. To "tap" the substance, rubber harvesters cut a V-shaped wedge in the bark. They have to remember to tap each tree in a slightly different place every time because repeated tapping in the same spot swiftly kills rubber trees. After workers make a cut, latex oozes out and collects in a container attached to the tree. Tapping takes place every other day, and each tapping yields about 2 ounces (56 grams) of the latex.

The Banbury mixer, which mixes rubber with other ingredients, was invented in 1916 by Fernely H. Banbury (1881-1963).

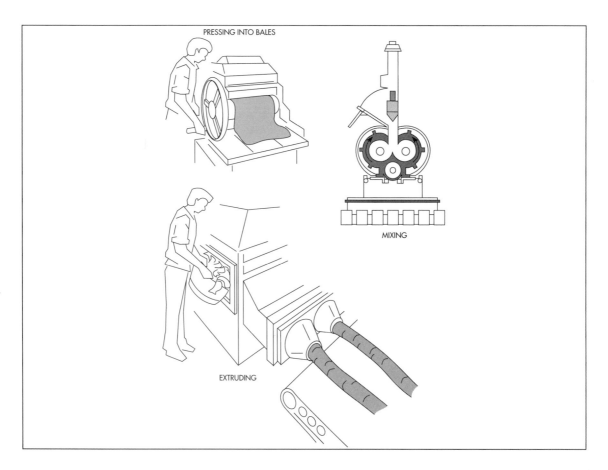

PRESSING INTO BALES

MIXING

EXTRUDING

Fig. 57. The rubber slabs are squeezed between rollers to remove excess water and then pressed into bales or blocks. These are cut into small pieces and mixed with other ingredients. Next, the heated rubber strips are fed into an extruding machine that forces the rubber out in long, hollow tubes.

Extrusion

6 After rubber leaves the milling machine, it is cut into strips. Still hot from the milling, the strips are then fed into an extruding machine (see fig. 57), which forces the rubber out in long, hollow tubes (much as a meat grinder produces long strings of meat).

Curing

7 The tubes of rubber are then forced over aluminum poles called mandrels, which have been covered with talcum powder to keep the rubber from sticking. Although the rubber has already been vulcan-

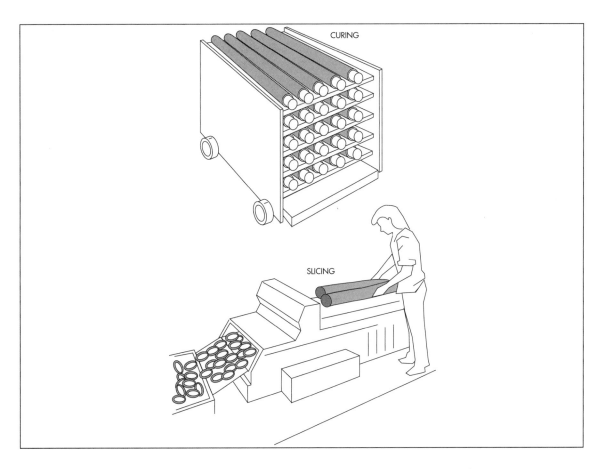

Fig. 58. After being extruded, the rubber tubes are forced over aluminum poles called mandrels and cured in large ovens. Finally, the tubes are removed from the mandrels and fed into a cutting machine that slices them into rubber bands.

ized, it's rather brittle at this point, and needs to be "cured"—its consistency changed to a more elastic state—before it is usable. To accomplish this, the poles are loaded onto racks that are steamed and heated in large machines (see fig. 58).

8 Removed from the poles and washed to remove the talcum powder, the tubes of rubber are fed into another machine that slices them into finished rubber bands (see fig.58). Rubber bands are sold by weight, and, because they tend to clump together, only small quantities can be weighed accurately by machines. Generally, any package over 5 pounds (2.2 kilograms) can be loaded by machine but will still require manual weighing and adjusting.

Rubber bands come in a variety of colors, shapes, and sizes.

Rubber bands not only hold together bouquets of flowers, but soft, loose rubber bands keep flower petals (especially tulips) from opening in transit.

Quality Control

Sample rubber bands from each batch are tested for quality in several ways. One test measures modulus, or how hard a band snaps back—a tight band should snap back forcefully when pulled, while a band made to secure fragile objects should move back more gently. Another test, for elongation, determines how far a band will stretch, which depends upon the percentage of rubber in a band: the more rubber, the farther it should stretch. A third trait commonly tested is break strength, or whether a rubber band is strong enough to withstand normal strain. If 90 percent of the sample bands in a batch pass a particular test, the batch moves on to the next test; if 90 percent pass all of the tests, the batch is considered market-ready.

Although most manufacturers sell rubber bands by the pound, some manufacturers will guarantee the number of rubber bands per pound. This added step not only assures quantity, but it also assures quality, due to the extra inspection the rubber bands get while being weighed and counted.

Rubber bands can be used to keep vegetables secure.

WHERE TO LEARN MORE

Cobb, Vicki. *The Secret Life of School Supplies.* J.B. Lippincott, 1981.

Gottlieb, Leonard. *Factory Made: How Things Are Manufactured.* Houghton-Mifflin, 1978.

Graham, Frank and Ada Graham. *The Big Stretch: The Complete Book of the Amazing Rubber Band.* Knopf, 1985.

McCafferty, Danielle. *How Simple Things Are Made.* Subsistence Press, 1977.

Wulffson, Don. L. *Extraordinary Stories Behind the Invention of Ordinary Things.* Lothrop, Lee & Shepard Books, 1981.

Smoke Detector

A smoke detector is a device that senses the presence of smoke in a building and warns the occupants, enabling them to escape a fire before succumbing to smoke inhalation or burns. Equipping a home with at least one smoke detector cuts in half the chances that residents will die in a fire. Smoke detectors became widely available and affordable in the early 1970s. Prior to that date, fatalities from fires in the home averaged 10,000 per year, but by the early 1990s that figure dropped to fewer than 6,000 per year.

There are two basic types of smoke detectors: photoelectric smoke detectors and the ionization chamber smoke detectors (ICSD).

Types of Smoke Detectors

Two basic types of smoke detectors are currently manufactured for residential use. The photoelectric smoke detector uses an optical beam to search for smoke. When smoke particles cloud the beam, a photoelectric cell senses the decrease in light intensity and triggers an alarm. This type of detector reacts most quickly to smoldering fires that release relatively large amounts of smoke.

The second type of smoke detector, known as an ionization chamber smoke detector (ICSD), is quicker at sensing flaming fires that produce little smoke. It employs a radioactive material to ionize the air (producing electrically charged atoms) in a sensing chamber; the presence of smoke affects the flow of the ions between a pair of electrodes (conductors), which triggers the alarm. Between 80 and 90 percent of the smoke detectors in American homes are of this type. Although most residential models are self-contained units that operate on a 9-volt battery, construction codes in some parts of the country now require installations in new

Smoke detectors may be installed on either ceilings or walls and should be placed near areas that are susceptible to fire, such as the kitchen or a fireplace.

homes to be connected to the house wiring, with a battery backup in case of a power failure.

Early Smoke Detectors

The development of these lifesaving appliances began in 1939 when Ernst Meili, a Swiss physicist, devised an ionization chamber device capable of detecting combustible gases in mines. The real breakthrough was Meili's invention of a cold-cathode tube that could amplify the small electronic signal generated by the detection mechanism to a strength sufficient to activate an alarm.

Although ionization chamber smoke detectors have been available in the United States since 1951, they were initially used only in factories, warehouses, and public buildings because they were expensive. By 1971 residential ICSDs were commercially available; they cost about $125 per detector and sold at a rate of a few hundred thousand per year.

This is the self-contained, battery-operated smoke detector most often found in residences.

Today's Smoke Detectors

A flurry of new technological developments occurred over the next five years, reducing the cost of the detectors by 80 percent and boosting sales to 8 million in 1976 and 12 million in 1977. By this time, solid-state circuitry had replaced the earlier cold-cathode tube, significantly reducing the size of the detectors as well as their cost. Design refinements, including more energy-efficient alarm horns, enabled the use of commonly available sizes of batteries rather than the hard-to-find specialty batteries that had previously been required. Improvements in the circuitry made it possible to monitor both the decrease in voltage and the build-up of internal resistance in the battery, either of which would trigger a signal to replace the battery. The new generation of detectors could also function with smaller

Smoke detectors are available in many forms, including one that screws into a 120-volt light fixture.

amounts of radioactive source material, and the sensing chamber and smoke detector enclosure were redesigned for more effective operation.

Smoke Detector Materials

An ICSD smoke detector is composed of a housing made of polyvinyl chloride or polystyrene plastic, a small electronic alarm horn, a printed circuit board with an assortment of electronic components, and a sensing chamber and reference chamber, each containing a pair of electrodes and the radioactive source material.

Americium 241 (Am-241), a radioactive material, has been the preferred source material for ICSDs since the late 1970s. It is very stable and has a half-life of 458 years. It is usually processed with gold and sealed within gold and silver foils.

Although ionization chamber smoke detectors have been available in the United States since 1951, they were initially used only in factories, warehouses, and public buildings because they were expensive.

The Manufacturing Process

The production of a smoke detector has two major steps. One is fabrication of the Am-241 into a form (typically a foil) that can be installed into the sensing and reference chambers. The other is assembly of the entire ICSD, beginning with all of the individual components or with prefabricated sensing and reference chambers obtained from the manufacturer of the radioactive source material.

Radioactive source

1 The process starts with obtaining an oxide of Am-241. This substance is thoroughly mixed with gold, shaped into a briquette (a small block), and fused by pressure and heat at over 1470 degrees Fahrenheit (800 degrees Celsius). A backing of silver and a front covering of gold or gold alloy are applied to the briquette and sealed by hot forging. The briquette is then processed through several stages of cold rolling to achieve the desired thickness and levels of radiation emission. The final thickness is about 0.008 inches (0.2 millimeters), with the gold cover representing about 1 percent of the thickness. The resulting foil strip, which is about 0.8 inches (20 millimeters) wide, is cut into sections 39 inches (1 meter) long.

2 Circular ICSD source elements are punched out of the foil strip. Each disc, which is about 0.2 inches (5 millmeters) in diameter, is mounted in a metal holder. A thin metal rim on the holder is rolled over to completely seal the cut edge around the disc.

The sensing and reference chambers

3 One disc of source material is mounted in the sensing chamber and another is mounted in the adjacent reference chamber. The electrodes are installed in both chambers and connected to external leads which project out of the bottoms of the chambers.

The circuit board

4 Printed circuit boards are prepared from design schematics by punching holes for the component leads and by laying a copper trace on the back to form the paths for electric currents. On the assembly line, the various electronic components (diodes, capacitors, resistors, among others) are inserted into the proper holes on the board. Leads extending out the back of the board are trimmed.

5 The sensing chamber, reference chamber, and an alarm horn are installed on the printed circuit board.

6 The board then passes over a wave solder machine, which solders (joins components together with melted metal) the electronic components into place.

Housing

7 The plastic housing consists of a mounting base and a cover. Both are made by injection-molding process in which powdered plastic and molding pigments are mixed, heated, forced into a mold under pressure, and then cooled to form the final pieces.

CAUTION, RADIOACTIVE

Although smoke detectors contain radioactive material, that doesn't mean they are health hazards. The amount of radiation they emit is well below the amount that could be harmful. As a matter of fact, a person would get more radiation from the carbon-14 that's naturally in the breath of a person sleeping near you than from a smoke detector in the same room.

There are smoke detectors available that have a strobe light alarm to alert hearing-impaired people of danger.

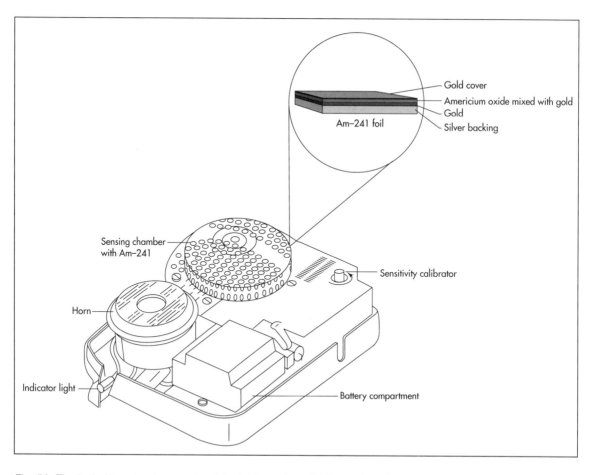

Gold cover
Americium oxide mixed with gold
Gold
Silver backing
Am–241 foil

Sensing chamber with Am–241

Sensitivity calibrator

Horn

Indicator light

Battery compartment

Fig. 59. The ionization chamber smoke detector is equipped with an alarm horn, a printed circuit board, and a sensing and reference chamber containing radioactive source material.

Tests and inspections at several stages of the assembly process ensure a reliable product.

Final assembly

8 The circuit board is seated on the plastic mounting base. A test button is installed so the device can be tested periodically after installation in the home. A mounting bracket is added to the base, and the cover is added to complete the assembly.

9 The smoke detector is packaged in a cardboard box, along with a battery and an owner's manual.

Smoke detectors wind their way down the assembly line.

Future Smoke Detectors

Some recent developments may make smoke detectors even more effective. One model, for example, uses a strobe light alarm to alert hearing-impaired people of danger. The remote strobe light can be mounted in a bedroom even though the detector may be located in another room or hallway, giving the same advantage of early warning available to hearing people when an alarm sounds from outside the bedroom.

In 1993, a smoke detector manufacturer redesigned a traditional smoke detector to fit in the standard air filters of a central heating or air conditioning system, in order to examine air that circulates through an entire building. When it detects smoke, the device shuts off the system's blower to prevent the air flow from helping spread the smoke and fire. In addition, it triggers an alarm that resonates through the duct work and is audible anywhere in the building.

Investigators at the Building and Fire Research Laboratory of the National Institute of Standards and Technology have found that various types of housing materials, such as wood, plastic, and drywall, make identifiable sounds as they expand from rapid heating. Piezoelectric (electric polarity caused by high pressure in crystal-like minerals) transducers (devices that works by using one source of power to create another) can detect those sounds even before the materials actually begin to burn. This would be especially helpful in detecting overheated electrical wiring within a building's walls, before a fire is underway.

WHERE TO LEARN MORE

Andrews, Edmund L. "Central System for Smoke Detection," *New York Times.* February 1, 1993, p. D2.

Kump, Theresa. "What You Must Know About Fire Safety," *Parents.* January 1995, p. 44-46.

"Listening for Hidden Fires," *Science News.* July 24, 1993, p. 63.

"Smoke Detectors: Essential for Safety," *Consumer Reports.* May 1994, pp. 336-39.

"Sounds Like Fire," *Discover.* May 1994, p. 16.

Soda Bottle

The soda bottle so common today is made of polyethylene terephthalate (PET), a strong yet lightweight plastic. PET is used for many products, such as polyester fabric, cable wraps, films, transformer insulation, generator parts, and packaging. It makes up 6.4 percent of all packaging and 14 percent of all plastic containers, including the popular soft drink bottle. Accounting for 43 percent of those sold, PET is the most widely used soft drink container. Aluminum, a close second, is 34 percent. Glass, which once was used for all bottles, is only a small percentage of soft drink containers sold today.

The strong lightweight plastic PET was developed in 1941, but it wasn't until the early 1970s that the plastic soda bottle became a reality.

History of Plastics

Plastics were first made in the 1800s from natural substances that were characterized by having chains of molecules. When these substances were combined with other chemicals in the laboratory, they formed products of a plastic nature. While hailed as a revolutionary invention, early plastics had their share of problems, such as flammability and brittleness. Polyesters, the group of plastics to which PET belongs, were first developed in 1833, but these were used mostly in liquid varnishes, a far cry from the solid, versatile form they took later. Purely synthetic (man-made) plastics that made a big improvement on earlier plastics arrived in the early 1900s, but they still had limited applications.

Early Soda Bottles

PET was developed in 1941, but it wasn't until the early 1970s that the plastic soda bottle became a reality. Nathaniel C. Wyeth, an engineer for the Du Pont Corporation and son of well-known painter N. C. Wyeth, finally created a usable bottle after much experimentation. Wyeth's crucial discovery was a way to improve the blow-molding technique of making plastic bottles.

Blow molding is ancient, having been used in glass-making technology for approximately two thousand years. Making plastic bottles by blow molding didn't happen until suitable plastics were developed around 1940, but production of these bottles was limited because of inconsistent wall thickness, irregular necks, and difficulty in trimming the finished bottles. Wyeth's invention of stretch blow molding in 1973 solved these problems, yielding a strong, lightweight, flexible bottle.

Soda Bottle Materials

PET is a polymer, a substance consisting of a chain of repeating molecules with great molecular weight. Like most plastics, PET is ultimately derived from petroleum hydrocarbon (an organic compound that contains only carbon and hydrogen). It is created by a reaction between terephthalic acid and ethylene glycol.

Terephthalic acid is formed by the oxidation of para-xylene, an aromatic hydrocarbon, using just air or nitric acid. Para-xylene is obtained from coal tar and petroleum through fractional distillation, a process that uses the different boiling points of compounds to cause them to "fall out" at different points of the process.

Ethylene glycol is derived from ethylene indirectly through ethylene oxide, a substance also found in antifreeze. Ethylene is a gaseous hydrocarbon that is present in petroleum and natural gas, but is usually produced industrially by heating ethane or an ethane-propane mixture.

The Manufacturing Process

Polymerization

1 Before the bottles can be made, the PET itself must be manufactured, or polymerized. In polymerization, smaller molecules are combined to form larger substances (see fig. 60). To make PET, terephthalic acid is first combined with methanol. This reaction produces dimethyl terephthalate and water. Next, the dimethyl terephthalate is combined with ethylene glycol at 305 degrees Fahrenheit (150 degrees Celsius) to form another substance, bis 2-hydroxyethyl terephthalate and methanol.

2 The final step involves the condensation polymerization of the bis 2-hydroxyethyl terephthalate. In this process, a polymer is formed while another molecule is released, or "falls out." The condensation polymerization of bis 2-hydroxyethyl terephthalate is carried out in a vacuum at 530 degrees Fahrenheit (275 degrees Celsius) and results in chains of PET and ethylene glycol (see step 1); the latter substance is continuously removed during polymerization and used to make more PET. After the PET mixture reaches the required viscosity (thickness), it is cooled to maintain product quality and to avoid discoloration. Later, it can be reheated for its various uses.

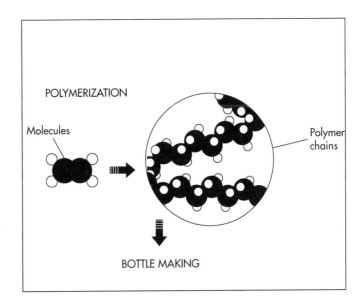

Fig. 60. In plastic soda bottle manufacture, the plastic—polyethylene terephthalate (PET)—is first polymerized, which involves creating long strings of molecules from smaller ones.

Bottle Making

3 PET beverage bottles are made using a process known as stretch blow molding (also called orientation blow molding). First, PET pellets are molded—heated and put into a mold—into a narrow tube of plastic, called a parison. The parison is then cooled and cut to the proper length.

4 Next, the parison tube is reheated and placed into another mold, which is shaped like a soda bottle, complete with screwtop. A steel rod (a mandrel) is slid into the parison (see fig. 61-A).

5 Highly pressurized air then shoots through the mandrel and fills the parison, pressing it against the inside walls of the mold (see fig. 61-B). The pressure of the air stretches the plastic both radially (out) and axially (down). The combination of high temperature and stretching in the desired direction causes the molecules to polarize, line up, and essentially crystallize to produce a bottle of superior strength. The entire procedure must be done quickly (because of the crystallization), and the plastic must be pressed firmly against the wall to avoid its being deformed.

Products made from recycled PET bottles include carpeting, concrete, insulation, automobile parts, clothing, and more PET soda bottles.

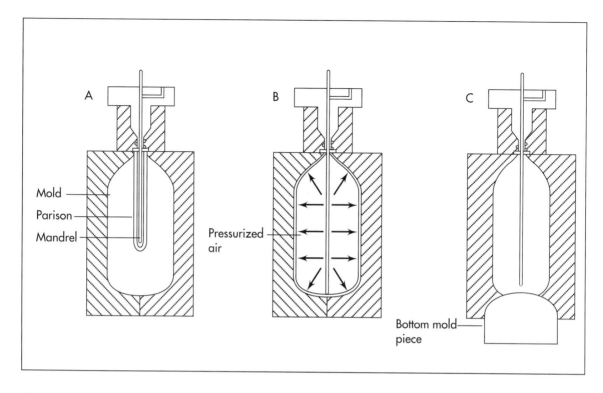

Fig. 61. In the process of blow molding, (A) a long tube (parison) of PET is put into a mold, and a steel rod (mandrel) is inserted into it. (B) Then highly pressurized air shoots through the mandrel and forces the parison against the walls of the mold. (C) A separate bottom piece is inserted into the mold to shape the bottle so that it can stand on a flat surface.

6 To give the bottom of the bottle its proper concave shape—so that it can stand upright—a separate bottom piece is attached to the mold during the blowing process (see fig. 61-C).

7 Next, the mold must be cooled. Different cooling methods are used. Water in pipes may flow around the mold, or liquid carbon dioxide, highly pressurized moist air, or room air can be shot into the bottle to cool it more directly. The procedure is done quickly, to set the bottle before plastic creep (excess flow) occurs.

8 The bottle is then removed from the mold. In mass production, small bottles are formed continuously in a string of attached bottles that are separated and trimmed. Other trimming must be done wherever the plastic has leaked through the cracks of the mold (like batter does

when squeezed in a waffle maker). Around 10 to 25 percent of the plastic is lost this way, but it can be reused in making more bottles.

9 Some soft drink producers make their own bottles, but usually finished bottles are sent by truck from specialty manufacturers to soft drink companies. Plastic is inexpensive to transport because it is light. Accessories such as lids and labels are manufactured separately. Occasionally, the plastic bottle manufacturer will put labels supplied by the soft drink company on the bottles before shipping them.

Quality Control

Polymerization is a delicate reaction that is difficult to regulate once the conditions are set and the process is in motion. All molecules produced during the reaction, some of which might be side effects and impurities, remain in the finished product. Once the reaction gets going, it's

During the polymerization and production phases of the soda bottle, the amount of acetaldehyde is monitored. Acetaldehyde can make soft drinks taste funny if it occurs in large enough amounts

impossible to stop it at midpoint to remove impurities, and it is also difficult and expensive to eliminate unwanted byproducts when the reaction is complete. Purifying polymers is a costly process, and quality is hard to determine. Variations in the polymerization process could make changes that are undetectable in routine control tests.

The polymerization of terephthalic acid and ethylene glycol can yield two impurities: diethylene glycol and acetaldehyde. The amount of diethylene glycol is kept to a minimum, so that PET's final properties are not affected. Acetaldehyde, a water-soluble, liquid, reactive compound, is formed during the polymerization as well as during the production of the bottle. It will give a funny taste to the soft drink if it occurs in large enough amounts. By using optimum injection-molding techniques that expose the polymer to heat for a short time, very low concentrations of

Rebecca Marcus, wearing a warm-up top made of DyerSport E.C.O, a fleece fabric knitted with Fortrel EcoSpun, hugs a tower of recyclable plastic soda bottles.

acetaldehyde appear and the taste of the beverage won't be affected.

Testing is performed on those specific characteristics of PET (consistency of size, shape, and other factors) that make it perfect for beverage bottles. For instance, PET must be shatterproof under normal conditions, so bottles undergo impact-resistance tests that involve dropping them from a specific height and hitting them with a specified force. Also, the bottle must hold its shape as well as resist pressure while stacked, so resistance to creep (the loss of material during the manufacturing process) is measured by testing for deformity under pressure. In addition, the plastic packaging must keep soda from going flat, or losing its carbon dioxide (the fizz in soda). Hence, the bottle's permeability to carbon dioxide is tested. Even its transparency and gloss are tested.

PLASTIC CLOTHES?

New Jersey-based Wellman, Inc. is the world's largest recycler of plastic bottles. One product it makes from the recycled bottles is a polyester fiber as thin as human hair, called Fortrel EcoSpun. Wellman knits the fiber into cloth that it sells to clothing manufacturers, who in turn make vests, jackets, sweaters, and even underwear out of it. It takes approximately 25 PET soda bottles to make one soft, warm polyester sweater. Twenty-five is not a large number, considering that Wellman recycles 300 million PET bottles a year and produces 15,000 tons of Fortrel EcoSpun.

Recycling

Many of the billions of PET bottles produced every year are thrown away, creating a serious environmental concern. Action has been taken to stem the waste flow, mainly in the area of recycling. Products made from recycled PET bottles include carpeting, concrete, insulation, automobile parts, clothing, and more PET soda bottles. Overall, bottle recycling is increasing, as is development of new ways to use recycled PET soda bottles.

WHERE TO LEARN MORE

Beck, Ronald D. *Plastic Product Design*. Van Nostrand Reinhold, 1970.

Modern Plastics Encyclopedia, 1981-82. McGraw-Hill, 1981.

"No Trash Talk for Polyester—It's Recycled," *National Geographic*. October 1994, p. 140.

"Picked Up, Dropped Off," *Beverage World*. August 1992, p. 16.

Sfiligoj, Eric. "Answering the Critics: Recyclable Polyethylene Terephthalate Beverage Containers Are Replacing Glass Bottles," *Beverage World*. June 1992, p. 34.

Wolf, Nancy and Ellen Feldman. *Plastics: America's Packaging Dilemma*. Island Press, 1991.

Sunscreen

The image of a healthy person today does not necessarily include a deep, dark tan. Research has linked exposure to the sun's ultraviolet rays to skin cancer, premature wrinkles, and other skin problems. While protective clothing such as hats, pants, and long-sleeved shirts are the most effective blocks against these damaging rays, sunscreen lotions also provide remarkable protection for the skin.

Ultraviolet Rays

Sunscreens are rated with a sun protection factor (SPF), which lets the consumer know how much protection against UVB rays the product provides.

The light emitted by the sun consists of three frequency bands of radiation: infrared, visible, and ultraviolet. Of the three, only the ultraviolet is harmful to most people. Ultraviolet (UV) radiation is further divided into three categories: UVA, UVB, and UVC. UVA radiation penetrates deeply into the skin's layers. This radiation has been linked to skin cancers and premature aging and wrinkling of the skin and causes sunburn. UVB radiation, which is stronger than UVA, is responsible for the painful, red burn people get after prolonged exposure to the sun. UVB rays also cause skin cancer and can damage the cornea and lens of the eye. The third category, UVC radiation, is generally absorbed by the earth's atmosphere and is not considered harmful.

Sun Protection Factor (SPF)

There are two basic types of sunscreen lotions on the market: products that penetrate the outermost layer of skin to absorb ultraviolet rays, and products that coat the surface of the skin as a physical barrier to ultraviolet rays. Both are rated with a sun protection factor (SPF), which lets the consumer know how much protection against UVB the product provides. The SPF of a product is the ratio of the time required for a person's protected skin to redden after being exposed to sunlight, compared to the time required for the same person's unprotected skin to redden. For example, SPF 15 means that a person whose unprotected skin would redden in ten minutes can apply the product and stay in the sun 15 times longer, or 150 minutes, before he or she gets a sunburn.

Researchers believed for a long time that UVB rays —the rays that actually cause a sunburn—were solely responsible for all forms of skin cancer. However, recent studies prove that UVA rays are also responsible. Although many sunscreens now contain UVA protectors, there are currently no standards set by the Food and Drug Administration (FDA) for protection against UVA rays. The SPF rating on a product applies only to UVB rays.

The FDA requires strict regulations and testing prior to the marketing of any new sunscreen lotion. Sunscreen producers go through an expensive and lengthy process to get FDA approval; this approval authorizes the manufacturer to produce the exact formulation applied for and is limited to only one SPF rating and one specific usage.

Development and Testing

Today's target markets for sunscreens are highly specialized. Sunscreen products are continually redeveloped to meet the changing needs of specific consumers. For instance, formulations for athletes may contain ingredients that are more waterproof and sweatproof, to provide protection for up to eight hours. Athletes may also desire a lotion that feels dry so as not to affect their grip. Children have more sensitive skin than adults because the outermost layer is thinner. This supports the find-

BURN TIME

To figure out how what number SPF to use, find your skin type and the amount of time you can spend in the sun without burning. Most people use SPF 15, which allows them to stay out in the sun 15 times longer than indicated below. If you want to stay out longer without getting burned, choose a higher number SPF.

Type O   *very pale skin*
           burn time: 1 minute

Type 1   *fair skin*
           freckles
           light-colored eyes
           burn time: 20 minutes

Type 2   *fair skin*
           red, blond, or brown hair
           brown eyes
           burn time: 30 minutes

Type 3   *medium-fair skin*
           dark hair and eyes
           burn time: 40 minutes

Type 4   *light brown skin*
           dark hair and eyes
           burn time: 50 minutes

Type 5   *brown skin*
           dark hair and eyes
           burn time: 60 minutes

Type 6   *dark brown or black skin*
           dark hair and eyes
           burn time: 75 minutes

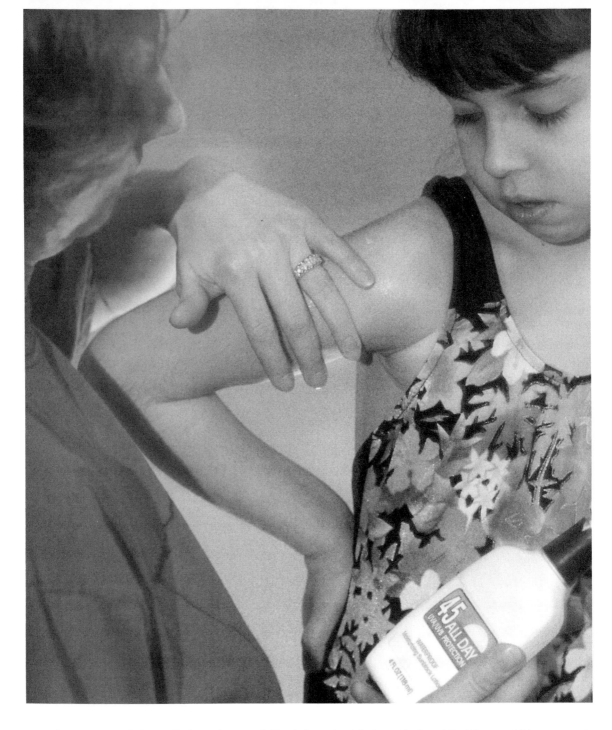

Applying sunscreen before enjoying outdoor activities is important, but people forget that they could be exposed to the harmful UVB rays everyday depending on the climate they live in. Applying sunscreen to all exposed skin as a part of getting dressed is becoming more commonplace.

ing that most sun damage to the skin occurs during childhood and the early teenage years. Sunscreens developed for the children's market tend to contain natural ingredients such as aloe vera and vitamin E.

In the development phase for a new sunscreen, a team of chemists and lab technicians develop the sunscreen formulation from synthetic and natural ingredients. Initial formulations are made in quantities of 10 gallons (38 liters), stored in stainless steel vats, and tested and finalized before an application for approval is made. FDA approval requires further testing which may be done in-house or by an outside laboratory. Examples of this testing include measuring the effective sun protection factor according to FDA guidelines, determining how safe the product is to use on the skin, and measuring the waterproof tolerance of a lotion.

VITAMIN D

Using sunscreen blocks the solar radiation that is needed for the body to make Vitamin D. But for most people, it takes only a few minutes of morning or late afternoon sun, two or three days a week during the spring and summer, to provide the body with many months' worth of vitamin D. Another way of getting enough vitamin D, especially for people who are housebound, is through food and/or vitamin supplements.

Sunscreen Materials

Many combinations of synthetic and natural ingredients may go into the formulation of a single sunscreen. A formulation is generally geared towards a specific SPF rating or the needs of a specific consumer group. Perhaps the best-known synthetic material used for protection against UVA rays is avobenzone, or Parsol 1789, which is used in products worldwide. Broad spectrum (comprehensive) protection is provided by other synthetic ingredients such as benzophenone and oxybenzone, which protect by absorbing UV light. PABA (para-aminobenzoic acid) was once a popular UV-absorbing sunscreen ingredient, but it can cause skin irritation in some people. For this reason it has been replaced by Padimate-O, a derivative of PABA. Other broad spectrum synthetic ingredients are octyl methoxycinnamate and menthyl anthranilate.

Titanium dioxide is a natural mineral and a popular ingredient for broad spectrum protection. Titanium dioxide works by scattering UV light instead of absorbing it. Although not as opaque as zinc oxide, it has a similar whitening effect in the higher SPF ratings. Antioxidants are often combined with titanium dioxide to slow down the oxidation of oils (breakdown of oil due to oxygen exposure) and thereby delay the deterioration of the lotion. Some examples of natural antioxidants are vitamins E and C, rice bran oil, and sesame seed oil. Another popular natural antiox-

People are exposed to ultraviolet radiation by the indirect rays reflected from sand, sidewalks, road surfaces, water, ice, and snow, in addition to the direct rays from the sun.

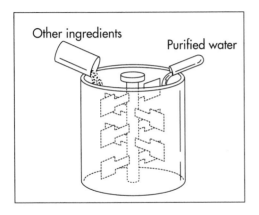

Fig. 62. Purified water and other purchased ingredients like avobenzone and aloe are mixed together.

Most sun damage to the skin occurs during childhood and the early teenage years.

idant is green tea. Many newer sunscreen products also contain skin soothing and moisturizing additives such as aloe and chamomile.

The Manufacturing Process

Sunscreen products may be manufactured, bottled, and shipped from a single facility, or portions of this work may be handled outside of the company. The fully automated manufacturing process described here uses some of both approaches.

Formulating the lotion

1 Water is purified using a method called reverse osmosis. Reverse osmosis extracts pure, fresh water by forcing water under pressure through a semipermeable membrane (a material that water can pass through) which separates pure water molecules from salts and other impurities.

2 Ingredients are purchased from outside sources and mixed with the purified water according to the recipe of the final formulation (see fig. 62). The recipe is recorded on a vat sheet which lists the exact measurements for each ingredient. Measurements are converted from the initial 10-gallon (38-liter) recipe used in the development stage to larger quantities for commercial use.

Making the containers

3 A blow molding facility manufactures the plastic containers for the sunscreen. In some cases this is done outside of the company. Blow molding is a method in which thermoplastics, plastics which soften when heated and harden when cooled, are extruded into a tube, called a parison, and placed into an open mold (see fig. 63). The mold is closed around the heated parison, and the parison is pinched at the bottom to form a seal. Compressed air is blown through the top of the parison which forces the softened plastic to expand to the inside walls of the mold, creating the shape of the container.

4 Containers are moved to a printing facility where logos and product information are printed, or in some cases stamped, onto the containers. Stamping embosses thin metal foil onto the surface of the con-

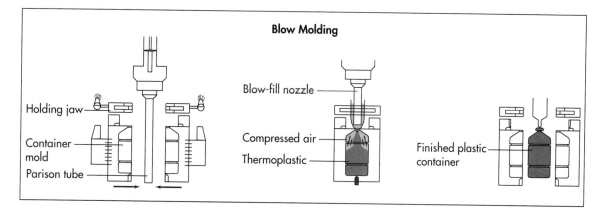

Blow Molding

Holding jaw

Container mold

Parison tube

Blow-fill nozzle

Compressed air

Thermoplastic

Finished plastic container

Fig. 63. The sunscreen container is made by a blow molding method, in which thermoplastic is extruded into a tube and blown into a mold.

tainer in the desired shape, usually a logo. The printed or stamped containers are then stored for use when needed.

Filling the containers

5 Stainless steel tanks with capacities up to 1,000 gallons (3,784 liters) are used in the filling process. Filling takes place in a separate, sterile room with a conveyor system of many incoming tracks. Machine operators monitor the automated process. Containers and caps enter the fill room on conveyor tracks. The sunscreen lotion flows from the vats through stainless steel piping to a pressure filling machine which inserts a retractable nozzle into each container and fills it with a measured amount of sunscreen lotion (see fig. 64).

Capping the containers

6 Most containers are capped automatically along the production line. Some containers include caps with pumps to allow easy dispensing of the sunscreen. These pump caps require manual assembly by operators as the containers leave the fill phase.

Shipping

7 The filled and capped containers are boxed in quantities of 12 to be placed on and secured to a skid (a platform used to support heavy objects) by shrink-wrapping for transport to distributors.

Sunscreen lotions that provide protection against both UVA and UVB radiation are known as having a broad spectrum of protection.

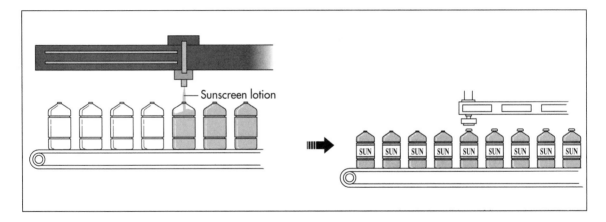

Fig. 64. The lotion is filled from stainless steel piping into each container. Most containers are then capped automatically and sent to distributors.

Reapplying sunscreen doesn't extend its protection, it just restores the original protection time.

Byproducts/Waste

Sanitized plastic scraps from the container molding process are reground and used again in molding. Containers that have been through the printing process and have flaws are passed on to other companies and made into products such as patio furniture.

Future Sunscreen

Researchers look to nature for the next wave in sunscreen development. Some plants have natural defenses against the damaging rays of the sun. For example, the single-cell alga called Dunaliella Bardawil that thrives in the Dead Sea and the Sinai desert makes its own sunscreen. Scientists at the Weizmann Institute of Science in Rehovot, Israel, have isolated the protein that this plant produces when sunlight gets too intense. The protein acts as a solar deflector by funneling light down to where photosynthesis takes place. Excess light that could interfere with photosynthesis is shunned by a yellow-orange pigment produced by the algae.

The human body also has a natural defense called melanin. Melanin is the brownish-black pigment found in skin and hair. It reflects and absorbs ultraviolet rays to provide a broad spectrum of protection. Dark-skinned people have a higher concentration of melanin and, as a result, have a lower incidence of skin cancer as fewer physical and medical signs of aging skin. Melanin was once painstakingly collected by extraction from exotic sources such as cuttle fish and cost about $3,000 per ounce

Sunscreen comes in various containers, such as these familiar plastic bottles.

($101 per milliliter). However, it can now be made in an inexpensive procedure using fermentation jars.

One method of incorporating melanin into sunscreen lotions is to encapsulate it into micro sponges that hold the melanin on the surface of the skin where it is most effective. The micro sponges can be seen only under a microscope. Researchers continue to gain approval for the many uses of natural and synthetic melanin as an ingredient in sunscreen formulations.

Sunscreen is now available in an easy-to-use pump spray, which prevents hands from getting greasy.

WHERE TO LEARN MORE

Brody, Jane. "Protection from the Sun: When a Little Isn't Enough," *New York Times.* June 14, 1995, p. C14.

Bylinsky, Gene. "Mass-Producing Nature's Sunscreen," *Fortune.* June 1992, p. 131.

"How Much Protection Is Your Hair Getting from a Leave-in Sunscreen?" *Glamour.* August 1995, p. 87.

"Putting Sunscreens to the Test," *Consumer Reports.* May 1995, pp. 334-39.

"Summer Sunscreen Special Report," *Zillions.* August/September 1995, pp. 34-35.

T-Shirt

T-shirts are durable, versatile garments that may be worn as outerwear or underwear. Since their creation in 1920, T-shirts have evolved into a $2 billion market. T-shirts are available in a variety of styles, such as the standard crew neck and V-neck, as well as tank tops and scoop necks. Their sleeves may be short or long, capped, yoked, or raglan (a sleeve that extends in one piece to the neckline). Additional features include pockets and decorative trim.

Since their creation in 1920, T-shirts have evolved into a $2 billion market.

Worn under a shirt, as a shirt, or over a shirt, T-shirts have become a wardrobe staple. That's because they are available in a rainbow of colors, patterns, and styles and fit just about anyone in any size, from infants to seniors. Adult sizes are generally small, medium, large, and extra-large, while sizes for toddlers are determined by age and weight.

T-shirts are popular garments on which to display one's interests, tastes, and affiliations using customized screen prints or heat transfers. Printed shirts may feature political slogans, humor, art, and sports, as well as famous people and places. They are also inexpensive promotional tools for products, places to visit, and special events.

T-Shirt Materials

The majority of T-shirts are made of 100 percent cotton, polyester, or a cotton/polyester blend. Environmentally conscious manufacturers often use organically grown cotton and natural dyes. Stretchable T-shirts are made of knit fabrics, rib knits, and interlock rib knits, which consist of two ribbed fabrics that are joined together. Jersey, a type of knitted fabric, is the most common material used to make T-shirts since it is versatile, comfortable, and relatively inexpensive. Jersey is also a popular material for applying screen prints and heat transfers. Rib knit fabrics are often used when a tighter fit is desired. Many higher quality T-shirts are made of durable interlock rib knit fabrics.

Neckbands add support to the garment and give the neckline of the T-shirt a more finished look. Neckbands are generally one-by-one inch rib knits, although heavier fabrics or higher quality T-shirts may require two-by-two rib knits. Neckband fabrics may be tubed (seamless) rib knits of specific widths, or flat fabric that must be seamed. Additional T-shirt materials include tape or seam binding, made of a twill or another stiff fabric. Binding reinforces the neckline and shoulder seams and, by covering the seams, it protects them from ripping apart under tension. Alternatively, elastic may be used at the shoulder seams so they remain flexible.

Two teenagers shop for T-shirts in a souvenir shop in San Antonio, Texas.

Thread is, of course, an essential element in sewing any garment. Several types and colors of thread may be used to make a single T-shirt. Some manufacturers use white thread for seams on all their shirts, regardless of color, thus eliminating the extra labor involved in changing the thread. Visible top stitching is done with a color of thread that blends with the fabric. Colorless, or monofilament, thread can be used for hems of any color fabric, again eliminating the need to change thread often (though monofilament thread may irritate the skin somewhat). Finally, optional decorative features may include trim, such as braiding, contrasting cuffs, appliques, and heat transfer or screen print designs.

Jersey, a type of knitted fabric, is the most common material used to make T-shirts since it is versatile, comfortable, and relatively inexpensive.

SUN-BLOCKING T-SHIRTS

*Exposure to the sun's harmful rays has become a concern to many people who enjoy outdoor activities. In addition to **sunscreen** (see entry) and sun glasses, sunblocking T-shirts are now available. SPF Wear Company in Chicago, founded by Harvey Schakowsky, has introduced a line of clothing, including T-shirts, that blocks out 93 to 99 percent of ultraviolet rays. A typical T-shirt blocks out only 50 percent of the rays. Using a fabric called Solarweave, these new T-shirts are made of synthetically woven nylon treated with a special chemical substance.*

Making T-shirts is a fairly simple and largely automated process. Specially designed machines integrate cutting, assembling, and stitching for the most efficient operations.

The Manufacturing Process

Styling

1 Once the T-shirt style is designed, the dimensions are transferred to patterns. Adjustments are made for size differences and stylistic preferences.

Cutting

2 The T-shirt sections are cut to the dimensions of the patterns (see fig. 65). The pieces consist of either a tubed body or separate front and back sections, sleeves, perhaps pockets, and trim.

Assembling the front and back

3 For fabric that is not tubed, the separate pieces for the front and back sections must be stitched together at the sides (see fig. 65). They are joined at the seam lines to form a simple, narrow, superimposed seam (made by placing one piece of fabric onto another and lining up the seam edges) and stitched together using an over edge stitch.

Assembling the sleeves

4 The hems of sleeves are generally finished before they are fitted into the garment, since it is easier to hem the fabric while it is flat. An automated system moves the sleeves to the sewing head by conveyor. The edge may be finished by folding it over, forming the hem and stitching, or by applying a band. The band may be attached as a superimposed seam or folded over the edge as binding.

5 If the T-shirt body is tubular, the sleeve material is first sewn together, and then set into the garment. If the T-shirt is "cut and sewn," the unseamed sleeve is set into place. Later during the final stage of sewing the shirt, the sleeve and side seams are sewn in one action.

Stitching the hem

6 The garment hem is commonly sewn with an over edge stitch, resulting in a flexible hem. The tension of the stitch should be loose enough to allow the garment to stretch without tearing.

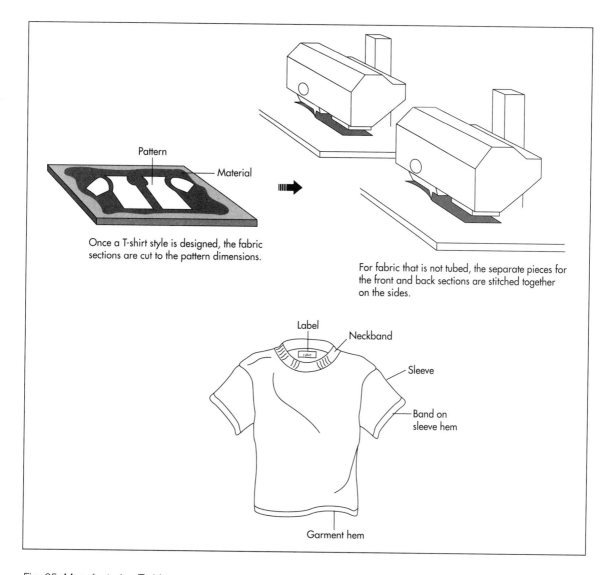

Pattern

Material

Once a T-shirt style is designed, the fabric
sections are cut to the pattern dimensions.

For fabric that is not tubed, the separate pieces for
the front and back sections are stitched together
on the sides.

Label

Neckband

Sleeve

Band on
sleeve hem

Garment hem

Fig. 65. Manufacturing T-shirts.

Adding pockets

7 Pockets may be sewn onto T-shirts intended for casual wear. Higher
quality T-shirts will have an interlining in the pocket so that it maintains its shape. The interlining is inserted into the pocket as it is sewn
onto the T-shirt front. Pockets may be attached to the garment with automated setters, so the operator only has to arrange the fabric pieces, and

T-SHIRT STANDARDS

Believe it or not, there are a number of standards to which manufacturers must adhere. Some of these standards include proper sizing and fit, appropriate needles and seams, types of stitches, and the number of stitches per inch. Stitches must be loose enough to allow the garment to stretch without breaking the seam. Hems must be flat and wide enough to prevent curling. T-shirts must also be inspected for proper application of necklines, which should rest flat against the body. The neckline should also recover properly after being slightly stretched.

Shirts are inspected by hand just before packaging. Those that don't meet manufacturing standards are sent back to be fixed, sold as irregulars to discount stores, or sold as rags to industrial companies, depending on the flaw.

the mechanical setter positions the pocket and stitches the seam.

Stitching the shoulder seams

8 Generally, shoulder seams require a simple superimposed seam. Higher quality T-shirt manufacturers may reinforce seams with tape or elastic. Depending on the style of the T-shirt, the seams at the shoulder may be completed before or after the neckband is attached. For instance, if a tubular neckband is to be applied, the shoulder seams must first be closed.

Attaching the neckband

9 For crew neck shirts, the neck edge should be slightly shorter in circumference than the outer edge where it is attached to the garment. Thus, the neckband must be stretched just the right amount to prevent bulging. Tubular neckbands are applied manually. The bands are folded, wrong sides together, stretched slightly, and aligned with the neckline. The superimposed seam is stitched with an over edge stitch.

Bound seams are finished with a cover stitch and may be used on a variety of neckline styles. The process entails feeding ribbed fabric through machines that fold the fabric and apply tension to it.

Some neckbands on lower-priced shirts are attached separately to the front and back necklines of the garment. Thus when the shoulder seams are stitched, seams are visible on the neckband.

V-necks require the extra step of either lapping or mitering the neckband. In the former process, one side is folded over the other. A mitered seam is more complex, requiring an operator to overlap the band accurately and stitch the band at center front. An easier method for a V-neck look is to attach the band to the neckline and then sew a tuck (fold) to form a V.

Finishing the neckline

10 Necklines with superimposed seams may be taped, so that the shirt is stronger and more comfortable. Tape may be extended across the back and over the shoulder seams to reinforce this area as well and to flatten the seam. The seam is then cover stitched or top stitched.

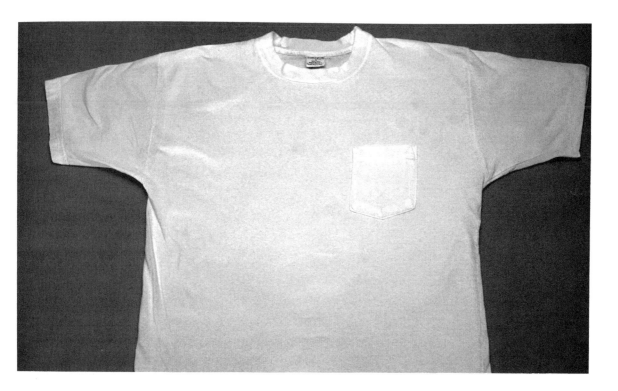

A plain white, 100-percent cotton T-shirt.

Label setting

11 One or more labels are usually attached at the back of the neckline. Labels provide information about the manufacturer, size, fabric content, and washing instructions.

Optional features

12 Some T-shirts will have trim or silk screen prints added for decorative purposes. Special T-shirts for infants have larger openings at the head. The shoulder seams are left open near the neck, and buttons or other fasteners are attached.

Finishing operations and packaging

13 High-quality T-shirts may be pressed through steam tunnels to get rid of wrinkles before they are packaged. Packaging depends on the type of T-shirt and the intended distribution

Taking T-shirts off the drying conveyor belt at a silk screening factory.

Higher quality T-shirts will have an interlining in the pocket so that it maintains its shape.

outlet. For underwear, the shirts are folded and packaged in preprinted bags, usually of clear plastic, that list information about the product. Shirts may be boarded, or folded around a piece of cardboard, so that they maintain their shape during shipping and on the shelf. Finally, they are placed into boxes by the dozen or half-dozen.

Quality Control

T-shirts are inspected for flaws in the fabric, stitching, and thread during the finishing process. Most of the operations in manufacturing clothing are regulated by federal and international guidelines. Manufacturers may also set guidelines for the company. There are standards that apply specifically to the T-shirt industry.

WHERE TO LEARN MORE

Callahan, Peter. "Sunday Best: Protective Wear for Your Day in the Sun," *Omni.* October 1992, p. 35.

Glock, Ruth E. and Grace I. Kunz. *Apparel Manufacturing: Sewn Product Analysis.* Macmillan, 1990.

Kopkind, Andrew. "From A to Tee," *Harper's Bazaar.* July 1993, pp. 34-36.

Solinger, J. *Apparel Manufacturing Handbook.* Van Nostrand Reinhold, 1980.

Traffic Signal

A traffic signal, or stoplight as it is also known, controls vehicle traffic passing through the intersection of two or more roadways by giving a visual indication to drivers when to proceed, when to slow, and when to stop. And, in some cases, traffic signals indicate to drivers when they may make a turn. It also signals to pedestrians when they may cross the street. Traffic signals may be operated manually or by a simple timer which allows traffic to flow on one roadway for a fixed period of time, and then on the other roadway for another fixed period of time before repeating the cycle. Some signals are operated by sophisticated electronic controllers that sense the time of day and flow of traffic to continually adjust the sequence of the signals. Traffic engineers use signals to avoid traffic congestion and improve safety for motorists and pedestrians alike.

The first illuminated traffic signal turned manually and consisted of two gas lamps, one red and one green. Shortly after its inauguration, however, it blew up, killing a policeman.

Early Traffic Signals

The first illuminated traffic signal was installed in London, England, in 1868. It was manually turned and consisted of two gas lamps, one red and one green, with semaphores (arms that change the position of the lights) atop a pole. Shortly after its inauguration it blew up while the lamps were being lit and killed a policeman. The first electric traffic signal was installed in Cleveland, Ohio, in 1914. It consisted of a green and red light with a warning buzzer to indicate when the light was about to change. The first signal to use the familiar green, yellow, and red lights was installed in New York City in 1918. It was operated manually from an elevated observation post in the middle of the street. In Los Angeles, traffic lights had green and red lights used in conjunction with a warning gong and a pair of semaphore arms lettered "stop" and "go."

Installed in Detroit, Michigan, in 1920, this was the nation's first three-color, four-way traffic light.

Today's Traffic Signal

A modern traffic signal system consists of three basic subsystems: the signal lights in their housing, the supporting arms or poles, and the electric controller. The signal lights and housing are known as the signal light stack. A single stack usually has three lights: a green light on the bottom to indicate that traffic may proceed, a yellow light in the middle to warn traffic to slow and prepare to stop, and a red light on the top to indicate that traffic must stop. Each light has a fresnel lens that may be surrounded or hooded by a visor to make it easier to see in bright sunlight. A fresnel lens has a series of concentric angled ridges on the outer surface of the lens, bending the light to focus it in a parallel beam. The light stack may have a dark-colored backing plate to make the signals more distinguishable by blocking out surrounding lights from buildings and signs.

There are one or more signal light stacks for each direction of each roadway. The electric controller is usually mounted in a weatherproof box on one of the corners of the intersection. More elaborate traffic signals may also have electromagnetic sensors buried in the roadway to detect the flow of traffic at various points.

Traffic Signal Materials

The housing or body of each signal light stack is usually made of corrosion-resistant aluminum. Some housings are molded polypropylene plastic. The lens for each light is tinted glass or plastic. The bulb, known as the lamp, is designed for long life and is purchased from a light bulb manufacturer. The bulb is partially surrounded by a polished metal reflector to direct the light forward. The hood or visor is aluminum or molded plastic.

The supporting arms or poles are usually made of galvanized steel for strength and corrosion-resistance. They may also be fiberglass. The controller is housed in a steel or aluminum enclosure. The electrical components within the controller—switches, relays, and timers—are purchased from various electrical component manufacturers. The wiring between the components is copper with a heavy neoprene rubber or plastic insulation.

The Manufacturing Process

A traffic signal is fabricated in the manufacturer's plant, then installed and wired at the site of the intersection.

Making the signal stack

1 The housing or body of each signal stack is die cast, as are the lens door and the bulb door that attach to the body. They may be cast as individual housings and doors for each light, or as larger units for

each stack. The die-casting process uses a large, two-piece, steel mold called a die. Inside the mold, called the cavity, is the reverse image of the part to be cast. The die is placed in a machine which clamps the two halves together with incredible force. Molten aluminum is poured into the "shot end" of the die, and a plunger rams the metal into the cavity under high pressure. The molten metal is forced into every portion of the cavity and cools. After about 15 seconds, the die is opened and the hot part is ejected. The part is then cooled for about 30 minutes.

2 Once the cast part is cooled, it is trimmed. The trimming process uses a stamping die to shear off any excess metal. The part is then visually inspected, and a hand file is used to remove any sharp burrs. The points where the doors are to mount to the housing are machined to ensure they will fit properly. The doors are attached to the housing with hinge pins and retained by spring latches. If the housings and doors have been cast individually, they are assembled to form the stack. The holes used for fastening the stack to the support structure are drilled. The stack is cleaned, painted, and placed in a drying oven.

3 The painted stack is transferred to a final assembly area where the lamps, lampholders, reflectors, and lenses are installed, using stainless steel screws and fasteners. The lenses are sealed against the lampholder assembly with weatherproof gaskets. The sheet metal visors, which were fabricated in another operation, are attached to each light. Wiring from each light is routed through the hollow stack housing to the stack mounting point.

This pedestrian traffic signal in Cologne, Germany, puts an emphasis on when NOT to walk!

Under normal conditions a die-casting machine used to make a traffic light housing can produce about 30 parts per hour.

Making the controller

4 The housing for the electrical controller may be cast or fabricated. It is trimmed, machined, and painted in much the same manner as the signal stack. Inside, it has mounting points to which the electrical control boards are attached. The traffic signal manufacturer may assemble the electrical components or may have this done by another company.

Making the supports

5 The supports may be cast, spun, or fabricated. Supports are hollow with an electrical junction box built into the base to connect with the wires coming underground from the controller. In some signal installations the light stacks are hung from heavy steel cables spanning the intersection.

Traffic signal supports include heavy cables and, as shown here, large poles across an intersection.

Some signal supports include decorative details to make the signals fit in with the architecture of the surrounding area.

Installation

6 Underground electrical conduits between the controller and each signal support location are put in place and connecting wires are pulled through the conduits. Power for the signal is brought to the controller location. If sensors are to be placed in the road, they are connected to the controller as well. The supports are bolted in place, and wires are pulled through the hollow supports between the base and the signal stack mounting point. The signal stacks are attached to the supports. The wiring is then connected between all the elements of the system. Each individual light is given a final adjustment to aim it properly, the sequence timers in the controller are set to the specifications determined by the traffic engineers, and the system is cycled several times to test for proper operation of each element.

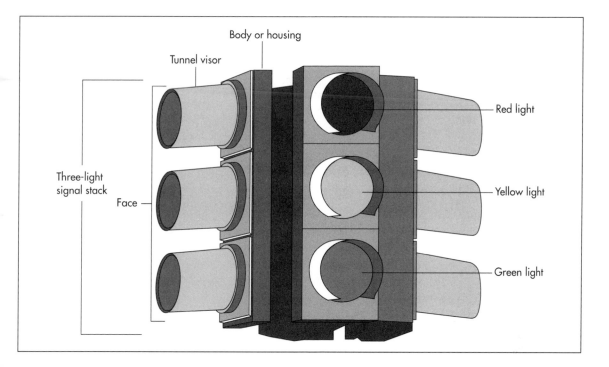

Fig. 66. Major components of a traffic signal.

Quality Control

The manufacturing process for traffic signals is subject to the standard inspections and control practices found in any similar production facility. These include both conventional and statistical methods. The installation on the job site must be reviewed by an electrical inspector from the agency placing the signal. Wiring must comply with the National Electrical Code. The location of the light and any other structural considerations must also meet various federal, state, and local regulations. A registered professional engineer must review and approve the plans to ensure the installation meets the national requirements for traffic control devices.

Future Traffic Signals

With the ever-increasing use of computers, traffic signals in the future will become more sophisticated. Many systems already feature a remote-controlled activation system that allows drivers of fire engines and other emergency vehicles to change the signal to green in their direction as they

GARRETT A. MORGAN

In the early days of the automobile, traffic control was a problem. Police officers tried to direct traffic and soon employed "Stop-Go" hand signs. However, as officers changed the signals with no advanced warning, motorists found themselves stopping in the middle of the intersection or coming to a near stop each time they approached an intersection. Either way, traffic did not flow so much as lurch along.

Garrett A. Morgan (1877-1963), an African American entrepreneur and inventor, experimented with automatic traffic signals in the early 1920s. His main innovation was the introduction of an intermediate position, the equivalent of yellow on a modern traffic light. This allowed motorists to anticipate a change and slow down only when necessary. Morgan sold his invention to the General Electric Co., which later made electric, three-light, four-way traffic signals.

approach an intersection. Some cities are developing networks of traffic signal controllers that interact to keep traffic moving through heavily congested areas or to reroute traffic during peak traffic hours. Other advances may include integrating speed warning devices and systems to check for stalled traffic or accidents.

WHERE TO LEARN MORE

"Braille Traffic Signals in France," *Wall Street Journal.* January 7, 1994, p. A4.

Brody, Jane. "Don't Walk, Run!" *New York Times.* March 23, 1994, p. C12.

"Keeping Traffic Signals Safe," *Weatherwise.* October 1993, p. 9.

"Let There Be Stripes," *Technology Review.* February/March 1994, p. 80.

Loggins, J.W. "New Traffic Signal Concepts," *Public Works.* March 1993.

Nadis, S.J. "Gridlock Terminator: Neural Nets Predict the Traffic Future," *Omni.* October 1994, p. 22.

Umbrella

The umbrella is primarily a device to keep people dry in rain or snow. Its original purpose was to shade a person from the sun (*umbra* is Latin for "shade"). Although people still use umbrellas to block the sun, these umbrellas are usually larger in size, such as a patio, golf, or beach umbrella.

Early Umbrellas

In art and literature from ancient Africa, Asia, and Europe, there are many references to umbrellas and parasols—a smaller-sized umbrella used as a sunshade, mostly by women. For example, the Egyptian goddess Nut shielded the earth like a giant umbrella—only her toes and fingertips touched the ground—thus protecting humanity from the unsafe elements of the heavens. Although the Egyptians used palm leaves and feathers for their umbrellas, they also introduced stretched papyrus (from the papyrus plant) as a material for the canopy, thereby creating a device that is recognizably an umbrella by modern standards.

About two thousand years ago, the sun umbrella was a common accessory for wealthy Greek and Roman women. It had become so identified as a "woman's object" that men who used it were ridiculed. In the first century A.D., Roman women took to oiling their paper sunshades, intentionally creating umbrellas for use in the rain. There is even a recorded lawsuit dating from the first century over whether women should be allowed to open umbrellas during events held in amphitheaters. Although umbrellas blocked some people's vision, the women won their case.

It was not until 1750 that Englishman Jonas Hanway set out to popularize the umbrella. Enduring laughter and scorn, Hanway carried an

In the first century A.D., Roman women took to oiling their paper sunshades, intentionally creating umbrellas for use in the rain.

In the late 1700s and early 1800s, another name for an umbrella was a "Hanway," named after Jonas Hanway, who popularized the umbrella in England.

umbrella wherever he went. Not only was the umbrella unusual, it was a threat to the coachmen of England, who derived a good portion of their income from gentlemen who took cabs in order to keep dry on rainy days. Braving similar ridicule in 1778, John MacDonald, a well-known English gentleman, also carried an umbrella.

Due to the efforts of Hanway, MacDonald, and other enterprising individuals, the umbrella became a common accessory. In nineteenth-century England, specially designed handles that concealed flasks for liquors, daggers and knives, small pads, and pencils, or other items were in high demand by wealthy gentlemen. The umbrella became so popular that by the mid-twentieth century, if not earlier, etiquette demanded that the uniform of the English gentleman include hat, gloves, and umbrella.

Umbrella Innovations

One of the most important umbrella innovations came in the early 1850s, when Englishman Samuel Fox conceived the idea of using U-shaped steel rods for the ribs and stretchers to make a lighter, stronger frame. Previously, English umbrellas had been made from either bamboo cane or whalebone. Rounded ribs and stretchers are seen today mostly on parasols and patio umbrellas, although some manufacturers produce umbrellas with these components.

Collapsible rain umbrellas that telescope into a length of about a foot are the most recent innovation in umbrellas. Though mechanically more complicated than stick umbrellas, they share the same basic technology. However, the collapsible version uses a two-piece shaft that telescopes into itself, and an extra set of runners along the top of the umbrella.

Umbrella Materials

The shaft of a stick umbrella is made of wood, steel, or aluminum, approximately 3/8 inch (.95 centimeter) thick (see fig. 67). Fiberglass and other plastics are sometimes used, and in fact are common in the larger golf umbrella. The ribs, stretchers, and catch springs (used to open and close the umbrella) are generally steel or other metal. The fabric of a good-quality umbrella canopy is usually a nylon taffeta rated at 190T (190 threads per inch), with an acrylic coating on the underside and a water-

and stain-resistant finish on the top. The manufacturer can either select patterns and designs from the fabric supplier or order customized ones.

The Manufacturing Process

Shaft

1 The first step in making a stick umbrella is to make the shaft (see fig. 68). The wood shaft is made using standard woodshaping equipment such as turning machines and lathes. Metal and plastic shafts can be drawn or extruded (forced through a die, or shaped hole) to create the proper shape.

Ribs and stretchers

2 Next, the ribs and stretchers are assembled. Ribs run underneath the top or canopy of the umbrella; stretchers connect the ribs with the shaft of the umbrella (see fig. 68). The ribs are attached to the shaft by fitting them into a top notch—a thin, round nylon or plastic piece with teeth around the edges— then held to the top notch with thin wire. The stretchers are connected to the shaft of the umbrella with a plastic or metal runner, the piece that moves along the shaft of the umbrella when it is opened or closed.

Different types and sizes of umbrellas are available, including this large-canopy umbrella and a smaller, collapsible version that is perfect for fitting inside purses or briefcases.

3 The ribs and stretchers are then attached to each other with a joiner, a small jointed metal hinge. As the umbrella is opened or closed, the joiner opens or closes through an angle of more than 90 degrees.

4 There are two catch springs in the shaft of each umbrella; these must be pressed to slide the umbrella up or down the shaft to open or close it. The metal shaft is usually hollow, and the catch spring can be inserted; in a wood shaft, a space for the catch spring must be hollowed out. A

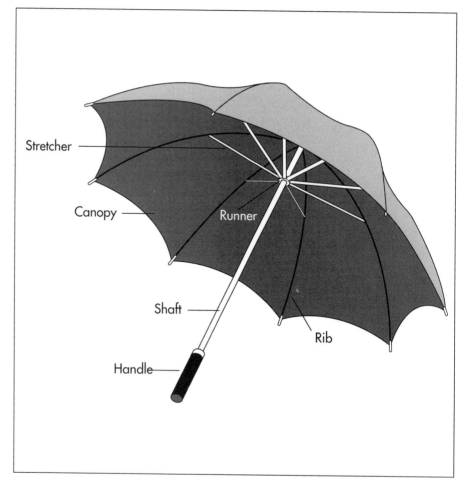

Fig. 67. The shaft of a stick umbrella is made of wood, steel, or aluminum. The fabric for the canopy is usually a nylon taffeta with an acrylic coating on the underside and a water- and stain-resistant finish on the top.

pin or other blocking device generally is placed into the shaft a few inches above the upper catch spring to prevent the canopy from sliding past the top of umbrella, when the runner goes beyond the upper catch spring.

Canopy

5 The cover or canopy of the umbrella is hand sewn in individual panels to the ribs (see fig. 68). Because each panel must be shaped to the curve of the canopy, the cover cannot be cut in one piece. Therefore,

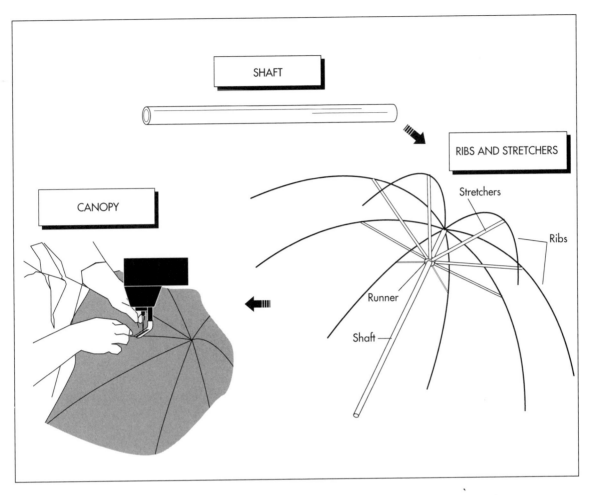

SHAFT

RIBS AND STRETCHERS

Stretchers

Ribs

CANOPY

Runner

Shaft

Fig. 68. The first step in manufacturing an umbrella is to make the shaft. Then the ribs and stretchers are assembled. Next, the nylon canopy is hand-sewn in sections.

each panel is cut separately from piles of materials called gores; machines can cut several layers at once, but hand-cutting is more typical.

Panels are then sewn at the outer edges of the ribs and between the ribs and the panels, about one-third of the way down from the outer edge of the canopy.

6 The tip of the umbrella that passes through the canopy is covered with metal (a ferrule) that has been forced over and perhaps glued to the tip, or left bare, depending on the manufacturer. The handle is connected to the shaft at the end of the process. Though handles can be screwed on, better-quality umbrellas use glue to fasten the handle more

He's singing in the rain with his trusty umbrella.

screwed on, better-quality umbrellas use glue to fasten the handle more tightly.

7 The end tips of the umbrella, where the ribs reach past the canopy, can be left bare or covered with small plastic or wood end caps that are either pushed or screwed on, or glued, and then sewn to the ends of the ribs through small holes in the end caps.

8 Finally, the umbrella is packaged and sent to customers.

Rain umbrellas are made with fabrics that can withstand a lot of water, dry quickly, and fold easily, and are available in a variety of colors and designs.

The typical rain umbrella has eight panels, although some have six (mostly children's umbrellas and parasols) or as many as twelve. At one point, the number of panels in an umbrella may have been an indication of quality (or at least of the amount of attention the umbrella maker paid to his product). Today, because of improved materials available to the umbrella maker, the number of panels is usually a matter of style and taste rather than quality.

Wacky Umbrellas

People will soon be able to keep their dogs dry in the rain with a new dog umbrella. This recently patented umbrella fits over the entire dog and stays on with a wide belt that wraps around the dog's stomach.

Another unusual product is the solar beach umbrella, which uses solar panels to power a fan attached to the umbrella's pole. That's what they call having it made in the shade!

Finally, a new golf umbrella on the market, called Fido (no relation to the dog umbrella), spans 62 inches, promises not to collapse against the fiercest wind, and sports a brightly colored ball retriever. This last feature is attached to a telescoping extension rod that extends up to 9 feet. It's perfect for those hard-to-reach balls, like the ones that land in the water or sand traps. Unfortunately, it doesn't improve one's golf game.

WHERE TO LEARN MORE

Crawford, T. S. *A History of the Umbrella.* Taplinger Publishing, 1970.

"How to Choose a Good Umbrella," *Consumer Reports.* September 1991, pp. 619-23.

"Nylon Ribs Toughen Umbrella Frame," *Design News.* June 16, 1986, p. 49.

Sedgwick, John. "Let It Pour: Getting a Handle on the Best Umbrella," *Gentlemen's Quarterly.* March 1992, p. 51.

Stacey, Brenda. *The Ups and Downs of Umbrellas.* Alan Sutton Publishing, 1991.

"Wacky Patents," *3-2-1 Contact.* June 1995, p. 18.

Violin

The violin is the most modern form of stringed musical instrument. It is crafted from various woods, contains four strings, and is played with a bow (a long wooden rod with horsehair stretched between two raised ends). Like the **guitar** (see entry in Series I) and other plucked string instruments, bowed instruments date back thousands of years. Although early violins were used for popular and dance music, they eventually replaced the viol as the primary stringed instrument in chamber music (music usually written for a small group of instruments) during the seventeenth century.

Most fine violins are still handmade by individual craftsmen using essentially the same methods employed by Italian artisans several hundred years ago.

Early Violins

Although its precise origins are not completely known, many people believe that the violin (and its larger siblings the viola and cello) evolved during the mid-sixteenth century in northern Italy. Andrea Amati (ca. 1500-77), often considered the first true violin maker, was also the leader of the Cremona, Italy, school of violin making. During the next 150 years, other members of the Amati family and their followers, including Antonio Stradivari (1644-1737) and Bartolomeo Giuseppe Guarneri (1698-1744), brought the violin to its highest level of perfection both as a musical instrument and as a work of art. During the seventeenth century, violin making spread to all of the other countries of Europe and, in the eighteenth and nineteenth centuries, to the rest of the world.

During his lifetime, Italian instrument maker Antonio Stradivari made about 1,200 stringed instruments. Of these instruments, only about 660 are thought to exist, including violins. A Stradivarius (the Latin name

"The Monasterio," a 1719 violin by Antonio Stradivari, was sold for £7,500 ($11,490 at today's conversion rates) during this auction at Sotheby's in London, England, in 1962.

Stradivari placed on his instruments) violin is considered by many to be of the finest quality. Its exquisite design and sound are qualities which many violin makers worldwide strive to duplicate. Musicians and collectors alike would like to own such a rare instrument, but for many people, a Stradivarius is out too expensive. Here's an example of just how much one is worth: in May 1994, four Stradivarius instruments were bought by a Japanese foundation for $15 million—that's $3,750,000 apiece!

Today's Violins

Violins have been and are being turned out by factories in Europe and Asia, but most fine violins are still handmade by individual craftsmen using essentially the same methods employed by Italian artisans several hundred years ago. People who want to become violin makers usually do so by becoming an apprentice (a person who works for no pay while learning a skill or trade). It takes several years to learn how to make a fine violin—a minimum of eight years to learn the craft and decades to master it.

This violin is only 1.39 inches long! Cornel Schneider, a Swiss craftsman, took 70 hours to build it using a dentist's drill, a scalpel, and other homemade mini-tools.

Tools

Most of the tools required for violin making are the same as those used for hand woodworking and carving: planes, chisels, gouges, knives, saws, and scrapers. In addition, a few specialized tools are needed, including a thickness caliper, small curved-bottom "thumb" planes, purfling groove cutter, peg hole reamer and matching peg shaver, bending iron, clamps of various types, and patterns. Many violin makers take pride in making some of their own tools. Indeed, one of the keys to success as a violin maker is developing the skills associated with making, using, and maintaining sharp-edged tools.

Straightness of the grain and the density and the figure of the wood contribute to the tone and visual beauty of the finished instrument.

Violin Materials

The back, sides (ribs), and neck of the violin are most often made of matching quarter-sawn (cut along the radius of the log) maple. The top of the violin is made of quarter-sawn spruce. The internal parts of the vio-

THE VIOLIN FAMILY

Ever wonder what the differences are among the viol, the viola, and the violin or the differences between a cello and a double bass? Basically, the viol has six strings (the violin has four), frets (ridges) on its fingerboard, is played with a curved bow, and rests vertically on the player's knee. The viola is slightly larger, tuned a fifth lower, and has a deeper tone than the violin. The cello, also called a violoncello, is much larger than the violin. It has four strings, is a pitch below the viola but higher than the double bass, and is held between the player's knees. The double bass, or contrabass, offers the lowest pitch and is the largest instrument in the violin family. Standing 6 feet high (1.8 meters), the double bass is also played between the player's knees. Like the other instruments in the violin family, the double bass is usually played with a bow, but its strings can also be plucked.

lin—the corner and end blocks and the linings—are usually made of spruce or willow, while the purfling (inlay) can be made of many different woods and/or "fiber"(thick paper or cardboard). The fingerboard is made of ebony (a black wood), the bridge is maple, and the other fittings (pegs, tailpiece, chin rest) are ebony, rosewood, or boxwood. Violin strings may be made of catgut (a tough thin cord made from dried animal intestines), catgut wound with metal (such as aluminum or silver), perlon, or steel. Rather than making these items from scratch, violin artisans usually purchase them in a finished or semi-finished form, customized or installed by the maker.

The Manufacturing Process

The ribs

1 The first step in making a violin is to make the ribs from which the outline of the top and back will be taken. The ribs are constructed on a mold, a wooden form cut to the exact outline of the inside of the violin. Pieces of wood for the corner and end blocks are cut to approximate size and temporarily glued to cutouts on the mold at the proper locations. With the aid of a pattern and using gouges and files, the blocks are trimmed to the final shape of the inside curves of the violin. Slices of maple slightly wider than the height of the ribs are cut and planed. Pieces are bent to the shape of the mold and blocks using a heated metal form. The ribs are then trimmed and glued.

To hold the ribs in place until the glue dries, molds shaped to match the outside curves of the ribs at the corners and ends are used. Pressure is applied by clamps or wrapping with string. Care must be taken to avoid gluing the ribs to the mold, which must be removed in another step. The ribs are glued in sequence starting with the middle bouts, which must be trimmed to final length at the corners before the upper and lower ribs can be added (see fig. 69). The linings, strips of willow or spruce are bent to shape using the bending iron, cut to length, and glued to the inside of the ribs. The corners are trimmed to their final shape, and the top and bottom surfaces of the ribs, linings, and blocks are planed and filed to be level at the final height.

Top and back

2 The tops of violins are almost always made from a wedge of wood which is cut or split, with the edges of resulting pieces glued together. This joint, for which the pieces must fit with absolute perfection, then becomes the centerline of the top. Maple for the backs of violins is treated the same way to make a two-piece back, although it is sometimes possible to find a piece wide enough to make a one-piece back.

Planing the wood to create a perfect center joint is an exacting task (see fig. 69). After the pieces have been planed to fit well—tested by holding the pieces together in front of a light—the edge of one piece is coated with chalk and rubbed against the mating edge. The areas in which chalk is transferred from one piece to the other identify places which must be shaved slightly with the plane to perfect the fit. This chalk fitting procedure is repeated until the fit between the two pieces is perfect, after which they are glued together and clamped.

After gluing the center joint, the flat side of the back and top are planed. The ribs are placed on this flat side; a tracing around the ribs enlarged slightly establishes the outline of the top or back (a square is added at the top of the back for the button). The outlines are then cut out.

The outside arching of the top and back are next carved using gouges, thumb planes, and scrapers for the final smoothing. Arching guides are consulted frequently as the plates take shape. The arching guides determine the design or model of the instrument. Most modern makers follow or copy the designs of great makers such as Stradivari or Guarneri, while some create their own patterns.

Next, the interior sides of the top and back are carved out. The final thicknesses of the wood has a major influence on the acoustic performance of the finished instrument. There are many systems used for arriving at the ideal distribution of thicknesses. In general, most methods involve testing the resonance (tone) frequencies of the plates by tapping or flexing and measuring the thickness of the plate at many locations using a graduation caliper. Then, depending on the results and on the desired outcome, wood is gradually removed from various locations.

The backs of violins are usually made using two pieces of wood, although it is sometimes possible to find a piece of wood wide enough to make a one-piece back.

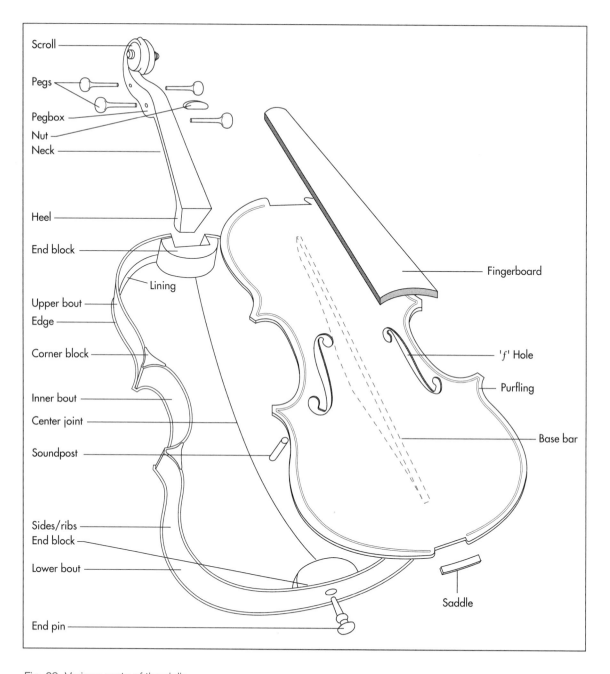

Scroll

Pegs

Pegbox

Nut

Neck

Heel

End block

Lining

Upper bout

Edge

Corner block

Inner bout

Center joint

Soundpost

Sides/ribs

End block

Lower bout

End pin

Fingerboard

'*f*' Hole

Purfling

Base bar

Saddle

Fig. 69. Various parts of the violin.

Completing the top

3 The outline of the sound holes is transferred to the top. The holes are usually cut out using a sharp knife, although some makers use a punch or drill to cut the round holes. The bassbar (see fig. 69), which strengthens the body, is made of very straight-grained, quarter-cut spruce. The area where the bar fits is outlined on the side of the top, and the rough blank is trimmed to precisely fit the arching. The chalk-fitting method is employed again in this step. The bar is then glued in place and trimmed to its final contour. This again involves testing the resonance of the top, which was altered by the cutting of the sound holes as well as the addition of the bassbar.

Completing the body

4 The mold is now removed from the rib assembly by loosening the temporary glue bonds of the blocks to the mold. The top and back are then glued to the ribs.

The groove for the purfling (see fig. 69) is marked a precise distance from the edges using a purfling cutter. The groove is deepened with a sharp knife and the wood in the groove removed with a purfling pick. The purfling strips, which can be bought ready-made or crafted by the violin maker, are bent to fit the groove using the bending iron. The pieces are then cut to the exact length, mitered to fit the corners, and glued in place. The channels which run over the purfling just inside the edges are cut with a gouge and blended into the arching with gouge, planes, and scrapers. Finally, the edge is rounded using knife, file, and perhaps sandpaper.

The neck

5 A block of maple matching the back is squared on the sides and top with a plane. Next, the outline of the side view of the neck and scroll (see fig. 69) is traced on the quarter-cut side of the block. The wood outside the outline is sawed away. Patterns and outlines for the peg box, top surface of the neck, and the scroll are traced. A razor saw is then used to cut away wood around the scroll and neck outlines. Gouges and scrapers are used to finish the carving of the scroll, the details of which are one of the ways in which the violin maker expresses his or her individuality. The pegbox is made using chisels and gouges.

The neck is cut to final dimensions using planes, knives, and scrapers. A mortise (cavity) to receive the neck is cut into the upper ribs, block, and top of the violin's body. The cut of the mortise and the root of the neck must be very precise, since the correct height and angle of the neck are critical to achieving a good tonal result. Chalk fitting is again employed. The neck is then glued into the mortise, and the final shaping of the heel of the neck and the button on the back is done.

Varnishing

6 Varnish is a coating consisting of resins (clear or yellowish-brown sap-like substances that repel water), which may be natural or man-made. Colored varnishes are made by adding pigments or dyes. The color of the individual coats may be varied to produce a desired appearance. Some people believe that secret recipes are responsible for the extraordinary tonal characteristics of the old Italian violins. Regardless of its possible effects on tone, varnish serves an important purpose by beautifying the appearance of the instrument and protecting the wood from wear, damage, moisture, and dirt.

Because there are many types of varnish and working methods, this general outline of finishing is provided. To darken the wood and bring out its shape, the violin is hung up to age (in some cases for several months or more) and may be exposed to sunlight. Many makers use other less time-consuming methods. After obtaining the desired color, a sealer or pore filler is applied. Next, varnish is applied in several coats. This process may include coats of clear varnish followed by additional coats of colored varnish. A final coat or two of clear varnish is applied to protect the layers underneath. The surface of the fully dried varnish may be rubbed out using some combination of abrasives (pumice, rottenstone, fine emery paper, etc.) and polishes. The part of the neck between the heel and the peg box is not varnished. Rather it is stained, sanded very smooth with fine emery paper and "french polished" (an application of shellac, and/or alcohol, and oil).

Fitting up

7 The top of the neck is planed flat, and the underside of the ebony fingerboard (see fig. 69) is planed to fit and glued in place. The sides and top are finished with planes, scrapers and emery paper to be smooth and to have exactly the correct curvature. The ebony nut is cut to size, lightly glued at the top of the fingerboard, dressed to final shape,

Etienne Vatelot in his Paris workshop. Not only is he France's master violin maker, he also repairs and tunes the instruments for such famous violinists as Itzhak Perlman and Isaac Stern.

and filed with grooves for the strings. A mortise is cut at the bottom of the violin into which is glued the ebony saddle. The pegs are shaved to the proper taper and diameter. Peg holes are drilled and reamed to match the pegs. Likewise, a hole at the bottom of the ribs is drilled, reamed, and fitted with the end pin.

The bridge and soundpost (see fig. 69) are the last parts to be fashioned; their fit and position greatly affect the sound and playing qualities of the violin. Starting with a precut blank, the feet of the bridge are cut to fit the arching of the top at the proper position—between the nicks of the sound holes. The top of the bridge is cut to an arch which matches the curvature of the fingerboard and provides the proper height of the strings. The front side (facing the neck) is planed down at the bottom and tapered from the middle to the top. Grooves for the strings are cut and filed using a gauge to establish their proper position and spacing.

The soundpost transmits the vibrations of the strings to the back of the violin. It is cut from a round piece of straight-grained spruce. Its

Many craftsmen believe that a violin needs 80 years of good playing to be broken in properly.

Since old-looking violins are more appealing to many players, some makers "antique" their instruments. The various methods of antiquing are usually trade secrets, and makers pride themselves on their individual results.

A violin should be so lucky. . . . This one ended up in the hands of violinist extraordinaire Itzhak Perlman who is really getting into his rehearsal for a series of upcoming concerts.

length and ends must be cut so that it fits precisely in the proper location inside the violin. The soundpost is inserted and its position adjusted through the sound holes. The strings are then fitted into the tailpiece, extended over the bridge and wound on the pegs.

Once all four strings are installed, they may be tuned up to pitch. What follows will be a period of adjustment as the violin becomes accustomed to the tension of the strings and their vibration. Numerous adjustments to the position of the soundpost, the bridge, types of strings, and perhaps other factors are usually necessary to optimize the tonal characteristics and playability.

Future Violins

It is likely that fine violins will continue to be handmade in the manner described above. There is a long history, however, of experiments with new designs and materials of construction. Recent developments include violins made of synthetic materials such as plastic. Some of these plastic instruments have solid bodies, while others are of a traditional design using synthetic materials for some parts. There are also electric violins, in which the vibrations of the strings are converted to an electrical signal by a pick-up or microphone, which is then amplified and output to a speaker or computer interface. There are a number of such "high tech" instruments on the market today, mainly used to play jazz and popular music. In the realm of classical music, however, the traditional violin is the dominant choice.

THE INDESTRUCTIBLE BOW

Violin students may no longer have to worry about damaging a bow while learning to play the violin. Traditionally, a violin bow is made from Brazilian pernambuco wood and strands of horsehair. When a bow breaks, a new one costs from $300 to more than $1,300. William Hayden, professor of violin at the University of South Florida in Tampa, created a durable bow made out of metal and chemically treated synthetic monofilament (manmade thread). Not only is Hayden's new bow almost indestructible, it only cost him $6.50 to make! Before he puts the new bow on the market, Hayden plans to refine his design.

WHERE TO LEARN MORE

Buchanan, George. *Making Stringed Instruments—A Workshop Guide.* Sterling Publishing Co., Inc., 1990.

Lipkin, Richard. "To Build a Better Violin," *Science News.* September 3, 1994, pp. 152-53.

"Rich Music from a Hardware-Store Bow?" *Science News.* June 12, 1993, p. 383.

Sacconi, Simone F. *The Secrets of Stradivari.* Cremona, 1979.

Yardley, Bill. "Moving Music," *Washingtonian.* October 1994, p. 218.

Index

Boldfacing indicates main entries; italicized numbers indicate series number

A

Axles *1*:4
Aztecs *1*:46

B

Bale chambers *2*:104
Baler pickup *2*:104
Ball bearings *1*:260
Balloon *2*:11-17, 38, 40, 50
Balm *1*:155
Banbury, Fernely H. *2*:227
Banbury mixer *2*:227
Bar code scanner *1*:12-19
Basalt *1*:201
Base notes *2*:200
Baseball *1*:20-26; *2*:19
Baseball glove *2*:18-25
Bearings *1*:142
Bedrock *1*:214
Beeper *2*:26-35
Bees *1*:18
Beeswax *2*:57, 62
Bell, Alexander Graham *1*:172
Benz, Carl *1*:2
Berthollet, Claude-Louis *2*:87
Besson, Gustave Auguste *1*:258
Bevels *1*:92
Bicycle *2*:36-47
Bicycle Museum of America *2*:38
Bidermann, Samuel *2*:213
Bifocals *1*:90
Billet press *2*:188
Binding *1*:37
Binoculars *1*:90
Bionic *1*:115
Biotin *1*:166
Black powder *2*:86, 89-92
Blanking die *1*:77
Blanking punch *1*:275
Blister pack *1*:78
Blow molding *2*:242-244, 252, 253
Blow torch *1*:261
Blown rubber *1*:194
Blue jeans *1*:27-35, 274
Blueprints *1*:42
Bluhmel, Friedreich *1*:257
Bombarding *2*:174-176
Boneshaker bicycle *2*:38
Book *1*:36-45
Bookmatching *1*:109
Bores *1*:243
Box tubular valve *1*:257
Box-stitching *1*:52
Brady, Matthew *2*:207
Braider *2*:52

Braille *1:*18; *2:*270
Brass *1:* 255, 256; *2:*21, 90, 91
Brigandine armor *1:*47
Broth *1:*63
Broyage *1:*69, 70
Bubble gum *2:*57-59, 63, 65
Budding, Edwin *1:*137
Bulb-wall blackening *1:*150
Bulletproof vest *1:*46-55
Bungee cord *2:*48-56
Bungee jumping *2:*48, 50, 51, 54, 56
Burn-in *2:*127, 219
Butting *2:*42
Buttons *1:*272
Bynema *1:*49

C

Cacahuatl *1:*63
Cadmium *1:*77
Calibration *1:*245
Calotype *2:*203
Cam *1:*75
Camera-ready *1:* 44
Cameras *1:*90; *2:*120, 127, 129, 202-207, 210-212
Candy *1:*71
Carbon *1:*121, 145
Carbon black *1:*247
Carbon rubber *1:*194
Carding *1:*30
Carnauba tree *1:*155
Cartwright, Alexander *1:*20
Carver, George Washington *2:*178
Casing in *1:*38
Casting *1:*122; *2:*136
Catcher's mitt *2:*18
Catsup. *See* Ketchup
Cavity *1:*256
Cayley, George *1:*116
CD. *See* Compact disc
Cedar *2:*187-189
Cello *2:*279, 282
Cello guitar *1:*108
Cellular phone *2:*33, 35, 82, 84
Cellulose *2:*205, 207
Celsius, Anders *1:*239
Cement lasting *1:*194
Central note *2:*200
Centrifugal pump *2:*75
Centrifuge *1:*225; *2:*15, 61
Chamois *1:*192
Charles, Jacques *2:*11
Chassis *1:*2
Cheese *1:*56-62
Chewing gum *2:*57-65, 89, 191, 193, 194

Boldfacing indicates main entries; italicized numbers indicate series number

Crepe rubber *1:*193
Crimping *1:*235, 260
Crucible method *1:*175
Crystallization *1:*226; *2:*243
Cuisine *1:*200
Curing *1:*249, 251; *2:*14, 20, 184, 228-229
Curtis, John *2:*57
Curtis, John Bacon *2:*57
Curve generator *1:*96
Cyanoacrylate glue *1:*230
Cylinder press *1:*37

D

Daguerre, Louis *2:*202, 203
Daguerreotypy *2:*203, 207
Daimler, Gottlieb *1:*2
Dassler, Adolph *1:*192
Davis, Jacob *1:*28
Davy, Humphry *1:*145
Deadbolts *1:*74
Deburring *1:*121
Defatting *1:*71
Degree of attenuation *1:*173
Denim *1:*27
Desktop publishing *1:*44
Dichromated gelatin *1:*14
Die-casting *1:* 278
Die-cutting *2:*9, 21
Diemer, Walter *2:*59
Differential speed mill *1:*168
Digital photography *2:*212
Directional solidifying *2:*136, 137
Disc-driven player piano *2:*216, 217, 218, 220, 222, 224
Dispersion *1:*105
Dixon, Joseph *2:*187
Dodge, Francis Despard *2:*195
Double bass *2:*282
Dry roasting *2:*181
Duco lacquer *1:*7
Dunlop, John Boyd *1:*246; *2:*38
Duryea Motor Wagon *1:*2
Dutch cocoa *1:*67
Dutching *1:*69

E

E. I. du Pont de Nemours & Co. *1:*48
E-coat *1:*8
Eastman, George *2:*204, 205
Eastman Dry Plate and Film Company *2:*205
Eau de toilette *2:*195, 196, 198
Ebony *1:*109; *2:*282, 286, 287
Edison, Thomas Alva *1:*146
Electric automobile *1:*11

Boldfacing indicates main entries; italicized numbers indicate series number

Electric guitar *1*:113
Electrodes *1*:145; *2*:107, 172-176, 233, 236, 237
Electroforming *1*:85
Electromagnetic induction *1*:210
Electroplating *1*:258, 262
Electrostatic painting *2*:108
Elongation *2*:230
Emulsion *2*:208
Endoscope *1*:173
Enfleurage *2*:196-198
Engraving *1*:185, 242
Environmental Protection Agency (EPA) *1*:242
Enzymes *1*:68
EPA. *See* Environmental Protection Agency (EPA)
Epoxy *1*:121
Erasers *2*:187, 190, 191
Essential oils *2*:195-197, 200, 201
Etching *1*:269
Ethylene vinyl acetate (EVA) *1*:194
Ewing, James Alfred *1*:210
Explosives *2*:86
Expression *2*:196-198
Extruder *1*:250
Extrusion *2*:51, 52, 228, 229, 252, 253, 273
Eyeglass lens *1*:89-97; *2*:66

F

Faber, John Eberhard *2*:187
Faber, Lothar von *2*:187
Fahrenheit, Gabriel Daniel *1*:239
Faraday, Michael *1*:210
FDA. *See* Food and Drug Administration (FDA)
Ferdinand II *1*:238
Fermentation *1*:68
Ferrules *1*:261; *2*:188, 191
Fiberglass *1*:48; *2*:266, 272
Fick, Adolf *2*:67
Filament *1*:126, 146
Film. *See* Photographic film
Filming *1*:41
Fire apparatus *2*:74, 75, 77, 78, 82, 84
Fire engine *2*:74-85
Fire truck. *See* Fire engine
Fireworks *2*:86-95
Fisher, Gary *2*:38, 40
Flaming cabinet *1*:160
Flash powder *2*:89, 91
Flashlight *1*:149
Flats *1*:41
Floppy disk *1*:98-106; *2*:216
Fluorescent inspection *2*:140
Fluorescent lamps *1*:147
Fluoride *1*:173
Flux *1*:261

Fonts *1*:39
Food and Drug Administration (FDA) *1:* 97; *2*:179, 180, 184, 249, 251
Ford, Henry *1*:1-2
Forging *1*:122
Formaldehyde *1*:165
Fortrel EcoSpun *2*:246, 247
Fortune cookie 2:96-101
Fractional distillation *2*:169
Fragrances *2*:193-196, 199-201
Frankincense *2*:57, 194
Freeblowing *1*:124
Freon *2*:2
Fresnel lens *2*:265
Frets *1:* 107; *2*:282
Friction inertial welding *2*:6
Functional testing *2*:140
Fuselage *1*:120

G

Galileo *1*:238
Galleys *1*:39
Galoshes *1*:273
Galvanometer *1*:210
Gama, Vasco da *1*:219
Geissler, Johann Heinrich Wilhelm *2*:169
Gelatin *2*:203, 204, 207, 209, 210
General Electric (GE) *2*:131, 270
General Motors (GM) *2*:51, 120, 124
Generator *1*:94
Genovese *1*:27
George Eastman House *2*:205
Gerbach, A. *1*:274
Germanium *1*:14
Gershwin, George *2*:216
Ginned cotton *1*:30
Glass *1*:84, 89; *2*:67, 196, 198, 203, 204, 266
Glass bottles *2*:162-163, 199, 241, 242
Glass tubes *2*:169-176
Glassblowing *1*:241
Glue *1*:229
Gold *1*:83; *2*:206, 236
Goldenrod *1*:41
Golitsyn, Boris *1*:210
Goodyear, Charles *1*:191, 247; *2*:226
Gore closure *1*:193
Granulator *1*:227
Graphite *2*:93, 186-191
Gravure *1*:42, 185
Gray, Thomas *1*:210
Grinding *1*:94
Gruentzig, Andreas *2*:16
Guarneri, Bartolomeo Giuseppe *2*:279
Guitar *1:* 107-114; *2*:279
Gum. *See* Chewing gum

Boldfacing indicates main entries; italicized numbers indicate series number

Gumballs *2*:62
Gunpowder *2*:2, 86, 87, 89
Gutenberg, Johann *1*:36

H

H. J. Heinz Company *2*:162, 168
Hagiwara, Makoto *2*:97
Hahn, Max *2*:131
Halftones *1*:41
Halide *1*:147
Hampel, Anton Joseph *1*:256
Hancock, Thomas *2*:11, 226
Hanson, Alden W. *1*:274
Hanway, Jonas *2*:271
Harness *1*:142
Hay *2*:102, 104-110, 195
Hay baler *2*:102-110
Heald, Jess *1*:25
Heart notes *2*:200
Heat blanching *2*:182
Heat test *1*:162
Heating-out process *1*:242
Helicopter *1*:115-127
Helium neon *1*:14
Heng, Chang *1*:208
Hershey, Milton *1*:66
Hetrick, John *2*:1
Highways *1*:10
Hittite *1*:107
Hobbyhorses *2*:36, 38
Hockey *2*:21, 111, 112
Holograms *1*:13
Holographic disks *1*:14
Holographic scanners *1*:13
Holstein cattle *1*:22
Hook-and-eye principle *1*:231
Houten, Conrad van *1*:66, 71
Howe, Elias *1*:272
Human-powered vehicle (HPV) *2*:46
Hydraulic press *2*:190
Hydrofluoric acid *1*:241

I

Ice skates *2*:111
Imposition *1*:42
In-line skates *2*:111-118
Incandescence *1*:145
Incandescent light bulb *1*:147
Incunabula *1*:36
Indigo *1*:27
Industrial robot *1*: 6; *2*:30, 31, 107, **119-130,** 138
Injection molding *1*:76, 86, 142; *2*:29, 69, 115, 237, 243
Inkometers *1*:44

Intaglio printing *1*:185
Integrated circuits *1*:82
International Museum of Photography and Film *2*:205
International Standards Organization (ISO) *2*:45, 206
Ionization chamber smoke detectors *2*:233
Iron oxide *1*:98
ISO rating *2*:206, 207

J

Jersey (material) *2*:256
Jet engine *2*:131-141
Joyner, Fred *1*:230
Judson, Whitcomb L. *1*:272
Jung, George *2*:97

K

Karman, Theodore von *1*:117
Kelly, Charlie *2*:38, 40
Kelvin, Lord *1*: 239
Keratometers *2*:67
Ketchup *2*:161-168
Kevlar *1*:48, 173; *2*:114, 133, 137
Kodak *2*:204, 205, 212
Krypton *2*:169
Kumax *1*:49
Kwolek, Stephanie *1*:48

L

Laboratory incubator *1*:206
Lacquer *1*:262
Laid paper *1*:184
Lands *1*:83
Laps. *See* Lens laps
Lappers *2*:70
Laser cutting *1*:84
Laser drilling *2*:137
Laser welding *2*:6
Lasers *1*:12, 80, 172; *2*:6, 32, 70, 107, 123, 127, 137
Latex *1*: 247; *2*:11-17, 50, 57-60, 227
Lathes *2*:273
Lavassor, Emile *1*:2
Lawn mower *1*:137-144
LCD. *See* Liquid crystal display (LCD)
Lead glass *2*:171
Leap pad *1*:94
Leather *1*:191; *2*:20-22, 24, 25, 41, 102, 111, 114, 194
Legumes *2*:178
Lenoir, Etienne *1*:2
Lens laps *1*:94
Lenses *1*:14
Lensometers *1*:93, 95
Leonardo da Vinci *1*:116; *2*:36

Boldfacing indicates main entries; italicized numbers indicate series number

M

Monroe, William *2:187*
Montgolfier, Jacques *2:11*
Montgolfier, Joseph *2:11*
Morgan, Garrett A. *2:270*
Morse, Samuel F. B. *2:207*
Mortar *1:200*
Mountain bikes *2:38, 39*
Mullen, Ernest *2:67*
Multimode *1:173*
Multiple-effect evaporation *1:225*
Museum of Electronics *2:30*
Museum of Neon Art *2:171*
Museums *2:30, 38, 171, 205*
Musical Instrument Digital Interface (MIDI) *2:216, 218, 221, 222*
Musk *2:195, 200*
Mycenaeans *1:46*
Mylar *1:101; 2:12*
Myrrh *2:193, 194*
Mystic Color Lab *2:211*

N

Nail polish *1:164-171*; *2:208*
Napoleon Bonaparte *2:87, 196*
National Food Processors Association *1:227*
National Institute of Justice (NIJ) *1:54*
National Institute of Law Enforcement and Criminal Justice *1:49*
National Institute of Standards and Technology *1:240*
National Optical Association *1:97*
Negatives *1:41*
Neon art *2:171*
Neon lamp *1: 147*
Neon sign 2:169-177
Neoprene *2:51, 81, 123, 266*
Neumann Tackified Glove Company *2:25*
Newton, Isaac *2:132*
Newton's third law of motion *2:131*
Nibs *1:69*
Nitrobenzene *2:195*
Nitrocellulose *1:165*
Nitrocellulose cotton *1:164*
Nomex *1:123*
NOTAR design *1:120*
Nylon *1:49, 75; 2:1, 4, 6, 9, 20, 41, 50, 51, 114, 258, 272-275*

O

Obrig, Theodore Ernst *2:67*
Offset lithography *1:42, 43*
Ohain, Hans von *2:131*
Olson, Brennan *2:112*
Olson, Scott *2:112*
Optical disks *1:82, 106*
Optical engineers *1:14*
Optical fiber 1:172-180; *2:176*

Boldfacing indicates main entries; italicized numbers indicate series number

Optical replication *1:15*
Optical system *1:17*
Ordinary bicycle *2:38*
Organic composite material *1:120*
Orientation blow molding *2:243*
Orthopedic running shoes *1:193*
Oscillation *1:211, 268*
Overlays *1:41*
Owens, Jesse *1:192*
Oxidation *1:145*
Oxide *1: 259; 2:1, 236, 242, 251*

P

Padlocks *1:74*
Pager. *See* Beeper
Paint *1:8; 2:43, 44, 78, 82, 108, 121, 125, 179*
Palmieri, Luigi *1:210*
Paper hygroscopes *1:44*
Papyrus *1: 36; 2:186, 271*
Parison *2:243, 252*
Pasteur, Louis *1:57*
Pasteurization *1:57*
Patents *1:28, 146, 257; 2:1, 11, 20, 58, 59, 111, 112, 114, 131, 187, 216, 226*
Peanut butter 2:178-185
Peanut oil *2:98, 182*
Peanuts *2:178-185*
Pencil *2:48, 51,* **186-192,** *225, 272*
Pendulums *1:207*
Penicillium roqueforti *1:62*
Penny black stamps *1:181, 182*
Perforations *1:188*
Perfume 2:193-201
Perinet, Francois *1:257*
Perkin, William *2:195*
Perlman, Itzhak *2:287, 288*
Perry, Thomas *2:226*
Persians *1:46*
PET. *See* Polyethylene terephthalate (PET)
Peter, Daniel *1:66*
Petroleum-based products *1:2*
Philately *1:185*
Phonographs *1:80*
Phosphor tagging *1:183*
Photo sensors *1:84*
Photodetectors *1:14*
Photodiodes *1:14*
Photoelectric smoke detectors *2:233*
Photographic film 2:202-212
Photography *2:202-205, 207, 212*
Photometers *2:181*
Photoresist *1:84*
Photosynthesis *1:220*
Piano. *See* Player piano
Piano action *2:213*

Boldfacing indicates main entries; italicized numbers indicate series number

Quilt-stitching *1:*52

R

Radiators *1:*5
radio frequency *2:*28
Radio-wave bulb *1:*153
Ramjets *2:*132
Ramsay, William *2:*169
Ransome, James Edward *1:*139
Rawlings Sporting Goods Company *2:*22, 24
Recalls *1:*10
Rechendorfer, Joseph *2:*187
Recycling *2:*211, 247
Reduced Injury Factor (RIF) *1:*25
Refining *1:*69
Relief *1:*186
Rennet *1:*56
Reservoirs *1:*241, 243
Resins *1:*49, 229; *2:*57, 63, 193, 195, 227, 286
Resonation *1:*107
Reverse osmosis *2:*252
Ribbon machines *1:*150
Riding mowers *1:*139
Riedlin, Joseph *1:*257
RIF. *See* Reduced Injury Factor (RIF)
Rivets *1:*28
Roasting *1:*69
Robot. *See* Industrial robot
Robotics *2:*30, 107, 119, 128-130
Roller mills *1:*157
Roller skates *2:*111
Rollerblades. *See* In-line skates
Rolling mills *1:*250
Roman Empire *1:*47
Rosewood *1:*108; *2:*282
Rotary mowers *1:*139
Rotary valves *1:*257
Rotary wing aircraft *1:*115
Rotors *1:*115
Rouge *1:*154
Rouletting *1:*188
Rounders *1:*20
Rowland Hill *1:*181
Rubber *2:*11-14, 16, 17, 29, 38, 48, 50-54, 57-60, 63, 71, 81, 105, 111, 112, 114, 123, 182, 187, 188, 225-232, 266
Rubber band 2:225-232
Ruhrman, J. R. *1:*274
Running shoe 1:191-199
Rupture testing *1:*162

S

Sabotage *1:*232
Saddles *1:*112

Safety pins *1*:272
Salsa *1*:**200-206**; *2*:168
Salsa cruda *1*:200
San Andreas Fault *1*:217
Sanctorius Sanctorius *1*:238
Sanforization *1*:32
Sanitation compounds *1*:97
Santa Anna, Antonio Lopez de *2*:58
Sargent, James *1*:74
SATRA. *See* Shoe and Allied Trades Research Association (SATRA)
Saws *1*:122
Sax, Adolphe *1*:258
Scale armor *1*:47
Scanners *1*:12
Schakowsky, Harvey *2*:258
Scheinman, Victor *2*:120
Schulze, Johann Henrich *2*:202
Screw press *1*:66
Scribes *1*:36
Scythes *1*:137
Seat belts *2*:1, 3, 10
Sechaud, Jules *1*:66
Sedimentation *1*:224
Seismograph *1*:**207-218**
Seismometers *1*:209
Seismoscopes *1*:207
Selective inking *1*:186
Semple, William F. *2*:58
Sewing machines *1*:272
Shackle *1*:75
"Shakey" *2*:119
Shannon, C. *1*:81
Shellac *1*:18; *2*:286
Shoe and Allied Trades Research Association (SATRA) *1*:199
Shoemaking *1*:196
Shubin, Lester *1*:49
Sikorsky, Igor *1*:117
Silica glass *1*:172
Silicon *1*:14, 267; *2*:30, 72, 98
Silkscreening *1*:242; *2*:262
Siloxane *2*:72
Silver *1*:83; *2*:87, 92, 202, 203, 205, 207-209, 211, 236, 282
Silver nitrate *2*:202
Skids *1*:120
Sloane, Hans *1*:65
Smoke detector *2*:**233-240**
Soda bottle *2*:**241-247**
Sodium lamps *1*:147
Solarweave *2*:258
Solder printers *2*:29, 30
Soldering *1*:256, 260; *2*:29-31, 219, 223, 237
Solenoid *2*:216
Solvent extraction *2*:196, 197
Solvents *1*:156, 164, 229
Soundboards *1*:108; *2*:215
Soundposts *2*:287, 288

Boldfacing indicates main entries; italicized numbers indicate series number

Toilet water. *See* Eau de toilette
Tomatillos *1:*200
Tomatoes *2:*161, 163, 165, 168
Top note *2:*200
Torque *1:*120
Touhy, Kevin *2:*67
Tractor *1:*139; *2:*84, 102, 104, 106
Traffic signal *2:*264-270
Transformers *2:*172
Transmissions *1:*5
Travers, Morris William *2:*169
Trumpet *1:*255-263
Tsung, David *2:*96
Tungsten *1:*147
Turbine blades *2:*133, 136, 137, 139
Turbine discs *2:*136, 139
Turbofan engines *2:*132, 135
Turbojet engines *2:*132
Turboprop engines *2:*132
Turning machines *2:*273
Twaron *1:*49
Two-dimensional bar code *1:*19
Tyers, Robert John *2:*111
Typeface style *1:*39
Typesetting *1:*38, 39

U

U. S. Post Office *2:*225
Ultrasonic testing *1:*142
Ultraviolet (UV) radiation *2:*68, 69, 248, 249, 251, 253, 254, 258
Umbrella *2:*271-278
Underwriters Laboratories (UL) *2:*176, 223
UV *See* Ultraviolet (UV) radiation
UVA rays *2:*248, 249, 251, 253
UVB rays *2:*248, 249, 253
UVC rays *2:*248

V

Vacuum deposition *1:*86
Vacuum evaporation *1:*224
Vacuum packing *2:*184
Van Wijnen, Wim *2:*46
Vapor deposition method *1:*173, 175
Vatelot, Etienne *2:*287
Vaults *1:*74
Vehicle Identification Number (VIN) *1:*10
Velcro *1:*49; *2:*114-116
Velocipede *2:*38
Veneer *1:*229
Vertical fiber drawing *1:*176
VIN. *See* Vehicle Identification Number (VIN)
Viol *2:*279, 282
Viola *2:*279, 282

Boldfacing indicates main entries; italicized numbers indicate series number